Failure

CW00823496

THE ART OF LIVING SERIES

Series Editor: Mark Vernon

From Plato to Bertrand Russell philosophers have engaged wide audiences on matters of life and death. *The Art of Living* series aims to open up philosophy's riches to a wider public once again. Taking its lead from the concerns of the ancient Greek philosophers, the series asks the question "How should we live?". Authors draw on their own personal reflections to write philosophy that seeks to enrich, stimulate and challenge the reader's thoughts about their own life.

Clothes *John Harvey*
Commitment *Piers Benn*
Death *Todd May*
Deception *Ziyad Marar*
Distraction *Damon Young*
Failure *Colin Feltham*
Faith *Theo Hobson*
Fame *Mark Rowlands*
Forgiveness *Eve Garrard and David McNaughton*
Hope *Stan van Hooft*
Hunger *Raymond Tallis*
Illness *Havi Carel*
Love *Tony Milligan*
Me *Mel Thompson*
Middle Age *Christopher Hamilton*
Money *Eric Lonergan*
Pets *Erica Fudge*
Science *Steve Fuller*
Sport *Colin McGinn*
Wellbeing *Mark Vernon*
Work *Lars Svendsen*

Failure

Colin Feltham

ACUMEN

Acumen Publishing Limited
4 Saddler Street
Durham
DH1 3NP

ISD, 70 Enterprise Drive
Bristol, CT 06010

www.acumenpublishing.com

ISBN: 978-1-84465-523-6

British Library Cataloguing-in-Publication Data
A catalogue record for this book is available from the British Library.

Typeset in Warnock Pro.
Printed by Ashford Colour Press Ltd, UK.

For Michelle, *der aldrig svigter mig*

Contents

Acknowledgements

I am grateful to the series editor Mark Vernon for responding warmly to my initial proposal and for helping to shape it, and to Steven Gerrard at Acumen for his constructive suggestions.

Friends who have through conversation and emails contributed wittingly or unwittingly to many of the ideas and examples in this book include Craig Draper, Jack Feltham, Geoff Haines, Michelle Hansen, Stephen Niechcial, Mark Saltiel, Virginia Sherbourne, Matthew Simpson and John Simpson-Smith.

By the rules of the game and the nature of the subject I am bound to state that any shortcomings, failings and errors in this text are mine alone – that is, unless they can be attributed to others' faulty texts, erroneous cultural memes, poor parenting, dumb genes, lousy theistic design or cosmic failure.

Introduction

Along with statements such as "You're fired", "I'm sorry to tell you that you have cancer" and "I'm leaving you", statements containing the word or concept of failure, such as "You've failed your school exam/driving test/job interview", probably rank clearly among the bleak negatives, or low points, in our lives. Small wonder that the subject of failure is not at the top of most people's favourites for dinner conversation, bedtime reading or even academic study. But I suggest that failure in one guise or another is pervasive, inescapable and has a great deal to teach us. On a personal level failure is usually success's ugly twin. Indeed, "unsuccessful" is synonymous with "failed". This book is not only about personal failure but this is one of its starting-points.

I hope this book comes across as authentically diagetic (from Plato's *diagesis*, the author speaking in his own voice), so let me give you a personal illustration. By some measures and in some people's eyes I am very successful. I am an early-retired university professor (indeed, the only person from my original wider family to have even gone to university) and I enjoy a fair amount of respect in my discipline and profession. I have written many books. I am loved, have good friends, family and two beloved sons. I own my own house and car and have enough money to live on. I have travelled fairly widely. I am in reasonably good health and have quite a bit of leisure time. In many people's fantasies I must be living the good life; certainly from the point of view of most people living in the developing world I am well off, well fed and very lucky. Few would call this failure.

However, we are raised to put the best face on these things and to conceal or play down the negatives. Like most lives, my life has had its good moments, successful spikes and peak experiences and periods of generally undisturbed well-being. But I have experienced depression and it's always there in the background, uncured by therapy. Like many people, however successful I may appear, I often feel a mere whisker away from failure. I have two divorces behind me and several "broken relationships". I became a professor quite late in the day, but in a subject that many regard as academically lightweight, and not the kind of high-status professor who brings in large sums of money for important research, sits on important committees and jet sets around the world. I became redundant about six months before starting this book and my pension is much more modest than that of most of my professional peers. My house is a small mid-terrace, my car is small and I can't really afford proper holidays. I often suffer from insomnia and am sometimes lonely. You could say that after some self-pity and adjustment at sixty, I have mostly come to accept all this. But my self-concept can shift from equanimity to a dark sense of failure. Maybe I can write quite well but can I sustain a very long-term relationship? I can write but I'm almost completely impractical. I can write but not as well as many others. And so on.

Perhaps you can already see two themes emerging here. One is that self-disclosure tends to feel a little embarrassing: one is aware that it isn't quite the done thing. Failure is stigmatic and parading one's failures may be considered unwise. The second is that personal success and failure are relative. There are implicit pecking orders. I *am* "more successful" than some people, even at close relationships! My income is better than many people enjoy, my Peugeot 207 is five years old, not six or seven, and so on. On the other hand it's pretty easy for me to think of friends in decades-long, happy-looking marriages. I know people whose income from pension schemes and other investments amounts to several times my income, whose house or houses are much larger and more expensive, who possess high-prestige cars and go on several annual holidays. I can certainly get eaten up with a sense of envy and failure. Alternatively, if I want to, I can think of one or two peers or individuals in a similar situation but who have less money but more *joie de vivre*, or who are more extraverted and attractive. I can also feel like a moral failure when I hear that a colleague has given up his car altogether for the sake of the planet.

A third angle emerges, then. Success and failure are open to interpretation. I could claim to have less than some people but to be wiser. I might tell myself and others that I have risen above acquisitiveness and envy, perhaps even above concern for personal comfort; that I am following the path of ancient Greek Cynics such as Diogenes in despising possessions, pretensions and the habit of clinging fearfully to life itself. Or I might, at any rate, allow others to believe that this is the case. To some extent it is true, I think, that I have rejected the accumulation of wealth as important and even, somewhat like Plato, consider it rather vulgar or even immoral. But partly this stems from having a socialist father and a shy, introverted personality. I have not been able to put myself forward for highly responsible work roles or to take business risks. So by one interpretation I might be "philosophically" successful, wise; by another I am a failure – I have never fulfilled my potential. This raises the interesting concept of mediocrity: I am neither a great failure nor great success, but sit somewhere in the middle. However, we know that "mediocrity" is associated with failure, at least by all-or-nothing measures.

Now, another perspective on interpretation is that we can focus on the individual who is considered to have failed at certain life tasks or to "be a failure", who has somehow failed morally to try hard enough; or we can look for other contributing factors. I have indeed already suggested something like this about myself, in my parentage and personality. Can we start claiming that our genes and upbringing are responsible for our failures? These are familiar claims. We can also begin to look at social, cultural, economic, educational and other systems' factors. How are the predisposing factors for failure laid down? How does schooling, for example, influence future success and failure?

This book is not only about personal failure, however, whether such failure is perceived subjectively or somehow measured objectively. However virtuous we may be, and however clever we become at extending the lifespan, every one of us must die of biological failure. Beyond individual lives, certain associated dynamics of failure can and should be investigated in society itself, in the human species and in existence itself. In other words, it is not a matter simply of the individual failing to be virtuous that we need to consider but the intermediate and largest ecosystems of failure, as it were. As in most houses, there are various parts of my house in disrepair. In a recent severe winter, the flaws of my central-heating system, lagging and draught-proofing were very evident, for example. In our increasingly technology-dominated lives we rely on appliances and communications devices that fail quite often. The screen of the laptop on which I'm writing this has turned an obstructive pink and needs a repair; my printer isn't working, ditto. All such items require maintenance, time and money: our so-called labour-saving culture frequently lets us down and demands even further layers of labour from us.

Most of us today live within capitalist systems and we are familiar with the flaws and occasional spectacular failures of free-market capitalism. Looking at the world of business, not even the most optimistic entrepreneur can deny that many small businesses fail in a relatively short time span and almost all businesses, however large and well established, eventually fail. Indeed, we may ask whether all human creations and institutions must sometimes falter and eventually fail, for example in the domains of engineering, marriage and religion. Nothing lasts forever, and entropy ensures that over time everything that we all hold dear will deteriorate, perish and disappear. Civilizations collapse, systems of knowledge become outdated and unbelievable; in some ways science makes certain aspects of religion redundant, as well as new scientific discoveries leading to the rejection of previous science; changes in society demand new moralities; social and medical improvements themselves (successes in their own right) create new demands on struggling health services and failing pension schemes; and so on. We have "failing schools" as well as failing pupils. Likewise some hospitals are deemed to be failing their patients and some social services departments are criticized for failing the children in their care when some of them are so severely abused by their parents that they die. All human life may be seen as a striving to overcome crises, adversities and imperfections.

But are there flaws in the non-human world? This question is important because we have some systems of belief and morality that tell us we are to blame for our own failures and for damaging our environment. We are sinful, fallen, alienated, flawed, and unable to appreciate and respect the beauty of the natural world, according to some religious accounts. Religion depicts a perfect God and/or a state of perfect enlightenment, and science the potential for perfect knowledge, against both of which we are seen as inadequate: not virtuous enough, not rational enough. However, it is not too difficult to point to flaws in theological and scientific theories and practices. Nor is it possible to depict all nature as good: wild animals must prey on each other and many suffer accordingly. Earthquakes, volcanic eruptions and tsunamis are all inevitable and in the long run we must expect some catastrophes, including the very long-term return of natural ice ages. And indeed, sadly, we know that the earth itself must one day perish, even without anthropogenic damage, as must the sun and the entire universe, however vast the timescales involved. Another name for all this is entropy, and I suggest that entropy is the inescapable template for all failure.

We are looking here, then, at everything from the smallest or most transient of failures (getting someone's name wrong, a social *faux pas*; missing a train; missing a penalty in a football match), through habitual failures such as addictions, personal cognitive errors and common epistemological fallacies, to large-scale and even ruinous social, ecological and cosmic failures. We are looking not only at obvious headline failures but also at the flaws and faults that may have been there all along, with the dramatic accident or catastrophe just waiting to happen, whether in human affairs or natural events.

Many of the examples of failure given in this book are interesting in their own right but inevitably we often examine failure in order to learn from it so we can improve matters in the future. Think of the notorious black box installed on aeroplanes. These flight (or accident) data recorders are considered crucial for discovering the causes of crashes. Educational and commercial endeavours commonly issue evaluation questionnaires to discover weak points and sources of dissatisfaction in the hope of remedying them and keeping on track with their pursuit of excellence. The very notion of progress seems to imply a relentless overcoming of obstacles to optimal personal and social health, wealth and happiness. Yet we know, and seem to want to know in our art and literature, that all is not well, that to err is human, that mistakes will happen and utopia will never materialize. We know, but do not like to dwell on it too much, that every one of us harbours ultimate biological failure.

Leave behind all hope of a Pollyannaish read, you who enter these pages. Forget that macho "failure is not an option" nonsense: failure is everywhere!

1. Origins, meanings and nuances of failure

Why does anyone feel like a failure? Where do we get our ideas from about the nature of success and failure? Why does failure sometimes seem so pervasive? And why do some philosophers find themselves having to begin their enquiries with topics of failure and disappointment? The contemporary philosopher Simon Critchley, for example, throws around these themes on the first page of his *Infinitely Demanding*:

> Something desired has not been fulfilled, ... a fantastic effort has failed. ... Absolute knowledge is beyond the ken of fallible, finite creatures like us. ... We seem to have enormous difficulty in accepting our limitedness, our finiteness, and this failure is a cause of much tragedy. (2008: 1)

For Critchley the failures of religion and politics are uppermost but here I shall begin our look at failure both more personally and more widely.

Let's hear Arthur Schopenhauer's head-on portrayal of human life as a failure:

> We begin in the madness of carnal desire and the transport of voluptuousness, we end in the dissolution of all our parts and the musty stench of corpses. And the road from the one to the other goes, in regard to our well-being and enjoyment of

life, steadily downhill: happily dreaming childhood, exultant youth, toil-filled years of manhood, infirm and often wretched old age, the torment of the last illness and finally the throes of death. ([1851] 1970: 54)

I shall unpack this dismal and entropy-focused account of specifically human experience further in Chapters 2 and 5. But let's keep in mind from now on the qualities and charges of madness, downhillwardness, toil, infirmity, wretchedness, torment and death that make this life resemble, for Schopenhauer, a penal colony rather than being a basis for human flourishing.

Some lucky souls seem to be born well, experience a minimal mismatch with their environment, thrive in love, work and health and have little use for failure as part of their vocabulary. Some are perhaps dominant and insensitive types who oppress and inflict failure on others rather than experiencing it themselves. But some of us experience painful dissonances, perhaps for a lifetime: friction with parents, failure at school, broken relationships, lots of struggle, poverty, illness and bad luck. As if it isn't bad enough to find yourself in this last category, when you cast around for comfort, explanations and solutions, the books, people and institutions you engage with may disappoint you; they may tell you success is in your hands and you are free to change or transcend your situation. Your thoughts, mood and personality could turn you towards religious hope for an afterlife, or towards suicidal depression, towards anarchistic anger and terrorism, towards an absurdist position such as that of Albert Camus or Samuel Beckett, the contemptuous pessimism of Schopenhauer, the stillness and insight of the Buddha, the amused nihilism of E. M. Cioran, or the Stoicism of ancient philosophers or modern-day cognitive behavioural therapists.

If, like me, you have a deeply sceptical disposition and a restless mind that is averse to belonging to any belief club, you may search for and be momentarily detained by nuggets of intellectual interest but the winds of doubt and nihilism sweep you ever onwards. Thinkers as diverse as Friedrich Nietzsche and Jiddu Krishnamurti have spurned the systematization of enquiry. A philosopher of art such as John Roberts argues that "the productiveness of the error in art operates *in defiance* of the programmatic, systematic or unitary ideal" (2011: 209). Stoicism, Cynicism and Epicureanism have their attractions but seem to demand inhumanly heroic ascetic actions and mental self-discipline that most us cannot command. Existentialism, similarly aligned with a personalized philosophy of living rather than the more abstract forms of philosophy, yet seems at least partly to fail the tests of my gut scepticism and of scientific data. A great deal of evolutionary, genetic and neurological essence surely does precede my own existence and limits my freedom. We may be time-bound beings facing death but we are also offered time transcendence by some oriental philosophies and religions, and "amortality" (Epicurean or otherwise) is currently a fashionable hypothesis. The Kantian club insists on moral value and effort in all circumstances, yet the recognition of contingency, of moral luck and pervasive tragedy, seriously challenges the Kantian position. Every philosophy, however attractive, is flawed. Indeed, Emmanuel Levinas famously and ironically declared that "the best thing about philosophy is that it fails" (Kearney 1984: 63).

Where should I look to help me understand failure? Simple introspection is one well-tried route. Anecdotal and objective evidence are further promising sources of aid. We might begin with an analysis of the generic concept of failure, or we might, like Michel Foucault, examine it via the lens of historical and contemporary culture. My epistemological radar picks up a variety of suggestive data. If we want to seriously investigate the fault lines that run through our own lives, we might allow that failure doesn't necessarily begin at home, in our own agency and culpability. Epicureans began their philosophical quests in cosmology and were far from alone in seeking patterns of behaviour that extend from cosmos to human being. Consider the following contemporary partial description of the formation of "our cosmic neighbourhood": "The asteroid belt between Mars and Jupiter consists of what is thought to be a failed process of planet formation. It failed, because the enormous gravity exerted by Jupiter would have torn apart any incipient planet that emerged in that area" (Spier 2011: 66). Cosmologists may now infer, then, that this asteroid belt was destined to become a planet but the process was aborted owing to greater inhospitable forces. Fallibility may be said to be an intrinsic aspect of becoming for *all* phenomena. It was not viable for this asteroid belt to become a planet in the circumstances prevailing so it became something else. One thing simply leads to another. For those who believe in God the creator, however, everything must have been designed to be what it was and is. God as an all powerful engineer could not have been thwarted by anything as trivial as enormous planetary gravity. God as an aesthetic perfectionist would not have settled for a failed process and outcome.

The same problems of inference are at work today when we ask whether a physically deformed baby was failed by God or destined by a quirk of fate to be different from the human biological norm; or if we are wrong to consider this baby "deformed" when it is simply different; indeed, whether our very perceptual and interpretative apparatuses oblige us to append labels instead of seeing and accepting "what is".

At one level we can infer that failure (or imperfection, or error) was an ever-present possibility; at another we shall insist that failure or imperfection is always about interpretation. Whether discussing an asteroid belt, the extinction of dinosaurs, a tsunami or earthquake that abruptly kills thousands, human diseases or one's own idiosyncratic struggles against adversity, we might say that these are all part of a richly diverse, unfolding cosmos and biosphere: ours not to reason why, the overall and ultimate design and purpose all in God's hands. The Hindu concept of karma offers an explanation of sorts for evolution and misfortune, based on adjustments for moral merit, but it is frankly not satisfying for all of us. Or some will say, even without God in the picture, that we must accept many things we do not like, respect differences and learn to improve where possible. For Plato, this world we inhabit is clearly imperfect and subject to decay, while in another, more real realm there is perfection. This of course parallels dualistic religious worldviews of "this life" (which is inferior and disappointing in some way) and a hereafter or heaven (which is perfect and a vindication). Also, we cannot ignore the question whether failure is the necessary and equal undertow of success in all matters or a mere sign of necessary risk on the road to inevitable success. Perhaps our utopian aspirations, always enmeshed with negotiations with failure, will eventually be realized.

The earth's environment is not a neutral ecology but one that generates considerable risk, cruelty, pain and premature death along the way. It may not properly be called a failure but it has its design flaws and we can at least imagine a world in which less suffering and failure was necessary. Herbert Marcuse (1987) made natural scarcity (or *Ananke*) a central plank in his argument concerning human repression and unhappiness. However much progress we have made as a species, and however much we personally aim for success and happiness and argue against determinism, we know we cannot evade some misfortunes. I am frankly dismissing crude creationist accounts here. One might simply say that they have failed to satisfy modern rational criteria for convincing explanation and have failed to adapt to evidence that has emerged since biblical explanations were created.

Homo sapiens has evolved from earlier primates. We have not by any means shed all the limitations or design flaws of our mammalian cousins; we have certainly made some improvements but we have also incurred some losses in the process, the most glaring being that probably very few of us could survive for very long in wholly natural conditions. Yet humans are often bedevilled by a sense that something preciously natural has been sacrificed in the course of our evolution towards cultural dependency. And to add to our discomfort, our existentialist philosophies suggest that we collude in lives of inauthenticity, bad faith and sickness unto death.

Before language no concept of failure-as-such can have existed for human beings but observations and experiences of failure in its broadest sense must have been common enough. Hunger, accidents, disease, predation, extreme weather and natural catastrophes, along with witnessing human deaths and rotting carcasses, would have signalled to our ancestors that all was not as they would wish it to be. However close to conditions of paradise early humans ever came, threats were never far away and vigilance was always necessary. Later, with the advent of agriculture and primitive technologies, humans would have begun to experience periodic breakdowns in their plans. Design imperfections led to learning to make improvements but all such efforts were, and remain, fallible. Language was essential in all this but it too contained flaws: words not yet invented, the birth of complex deception and misunderstanding. Vigilance, planning and the drive to survive and succeed have been constant; but equally entropy has been ever present: our best-laid plans are always subject to breakdown. We can argue that humanity intends to improve (succeeding and failing in due proportion) on natural hazardousness but that nature is indifferent. Willem Drees's book *Is Nature Ever Evil?* (2003) provides copious examples of exactly how "evil" or flawed nature is. The reversal of an anthropathological or original sin account might be that nature is often blind, inefficient and cruel and the human being, however fallible, will gradually overcome these original flaws of nature. Indeed, this is the standard scientific and optimistic science-fiction view: we will anticipate earthquakes, asteroids and drought, and bio-colonize currently barren planets.

Early theologies refined narrative accounts of the causal chain between the omnipotent God's perfect creation and humans' disobedience, which brought original sin, suffering and death into existence. Hindu theology offered causal (karmic) explanations for suffering in relation to the many natural forms in creation. Buddhism identified suffering as a universal phenomenon, closely linked with human desire and dissatisfaction. Early philosophers – the Presocratics, Socrates, Plato and others – began to focus more closely and logically on human agency and human institutions in their imperfect and improvable forms. Concepts similar to sin (*hamartia*, tragic flaw, or missing the mark, and *akrasia*, weakness of will) arose. With Aristotle came the beginnings of formal knowledge and science. All subsequent philosophy has sought to improve on the understanding of previous philosophy and, along with science, has gradually eroded many religious views. Yet all attempts at perfect understanding and knowledge are fallible, all limited by human intelligence. Curiosity necessarily entails enquiry into how and why things go wrong or are not in line with our wishes or certainties. Human beings have been driven by their environment and consciousness to discover reasons for existence, injustice, sin (or error, or failure), evil and death, among other challenges.

In my own view, religious explanations for the human condition have had their place but their credibility decreases steadily with the rise of much more compelling explanations. Ultimately, religion fails to explain human development and behaviour and appears not to be capable of correcting it; indeed, it may add to our flaws. Philosophy, relying on reason, has been freer to consider other explanations but it too often fails in many ways to show its relevance or potency, operating instead as if detached from brute reality. Postmodernist writers tell us that no one can legitimately pronounce on life as if disembodied, with "a view from nowhere", but we persist in such detached exercises.

I realize even as I write these words, however, that the intellectual terrain is so extensive that neither I nor (probably) anyone else can have the expertise to grasp all the data accurately. We all have imperfect or flawed intellects and academic research and its jargon becomes more specialized by the day. Our tendency is to multiply theories, hang on to redundant theories and fiercely defend our own self-serving theories against others rather than seriously attempt rapprochement (we have marked epistemological failures) and all human knowledge is fallible and ever changing. Science itself is flawed in spite of its remarkable discoveries: like all human endeavours, science goes wrong, as evidenced in accidents, ethical breaches, fraud, misappropriation of dangerous findings and products. Also, as Simon LeVay puts it, "for every brilliant scientific success there are a dozen failures" (2009: vii). Far more than a dozen, one would think. But many sciences, and some humanities subjects, generate new material evidence and hypotheses that far surpass the backward-looking nature of so much theology and some philosophy.

There are many names for our human folly and destructiveness, from original sin and evil to alienation, universal neurosis and "man's inhumanity to man". There is much speculation, and always has been among theologians and philosophers, about the origins and causes of, and possible remedies for, our ills. *"Unde hoc malum?"* Where does this wrongdoing come from? The question is an old one (Jacobs 2008: xv). We can, I believe, paraphrase this with no loss or distortion of meaning as "Where do our pervasive moral flaws and associated shared failures come from?" Academics are arguably obsessed with points of evidence, detail and classification, which tend to narrow enquiry into slow-moving, discipline-specific channels and prevent broad, socially significant and urgent enquiry and remedies. Put differently, the scholarly tradition stemming from Aristotle fails to appreciate and address the enormity and urgency of the question, and it too often gets left to an unsatisfactory mixture of folk psychology and religious opinion and dogma.

Here I perhaps need to insert a plea for patience. I am very aware from a psychotherapeutic perspective that most individuals want explanations for what they assume is their own unique form of suffering and, even more than this, they crave solutions. Quite naturally we are chiefly concerned with our own environment and being but in this regard we are often somewhat myopic. While we may demand that any therapy or philosophy of living should yield short-term personal dividends, we risk failed understanding if we impatiently dismiss explanations that place the "unique me" and contemporary humanity in the deepest context of evolution and history. This is not mere historical waffle but an account that lives on in us in our genes and behaviour. Schopenhauer did not have sophisticated cosmological and evolutionary data available to him with which to investigate the possible origins of our human condition and even until quite recently many philosophers have shied away from engagement with Darwinian themes. The foundations of much Western philosophy lie in and require a faith in reason as cerebral freedom and an aversion to anything that implies we are determined by brute forces and have only illusory freedoms. Eastern traditions are arguably more comfortable with concepts of fatalism and illusion.

Evolutionary psychology and its incipient applied forms of psychiatry and psychotherapy argue that many of our stubborn, self-defeating traits result from deep-seated behavioural orientations laid down thousands of years ago. We evolved like all animals needing food and sex for survival. We evolved in small groups heavily reliant on social factors. Some degree of natural territoriality, kin preference, xenophobia, aggression, gender-role division, leadership and subordinate roles is inherent in our nature. We did not evolve to be entirely trusting, altruistic, cooperative, rational and so on, and we have difficulty adapting to modern lifestyles.

Obviously we have adapted a great deal over thousands of years but we cannot shake off certain "primitive drives". We evolved physically by slow adaptation from existing anatomical foundations. For example, our mammalian ancestors walked on all fours and the human spine has that same original purpose. We have succeeded in walking upright but the common backache attests to our imperfect design, and there are many more examples of a mismatch between our origins and our current behaviour. Gary Marcus (2008) refers to all such mismatching features as "kluges" (an engineering term referring to clumsy but once-effective solutions to problems of adaptation) and sees no reason to draw a barrier between physical and mental evolutionary mismatches. The point is that all such imperfect adaptations form the basis of human flaws and failures.

There is considerable agreement among cognitive psychologists and some philosophers that many of our common perceptions, beliefs and behaviours are based on flaws in thinking and even physiology. We rarely see what is actually in our visual field but an edited version of it, owing to blinking, limitations of the fovea (where visual acuity is far greatest), saccades (necessarily jerky eye movements) and general inattention. We like to believe we are fair-minded and make good judgements, a majority believing, for example, that we are better than average drivers, more competent than others, more reliable and so on: all these are known as egotistic illusions. Psychological experiments seem to demonstrate repeatedly what distorted memories we have: "over the past three decades psychologists have demonstrated beyond any doubt that memory is staggeringly fallible and suggestible" (Lawton 2011: 39). Similar observations extend to serious doubts about the existence of free will. Yet, it is argued, we need all such illusions to maintain our sense of integrity and executive control.

Such hypotheses are hard to prove and much disliked within liberal cultures. The very assertion of anything that smacks of "determinism" can call forth vitriolic criticism. These kinds of hypothesis seem to suggest that human nature is intractable and worthy of only the most pessimistic of expectations. Critics point to copious examples of human goodness and creativity, underpinned by burgeoning theories of neuroplasticity, social learning, positive psychology and human flourishing, to dismiss evolutionary mismatch accounts. Or certain political philosophers and sociologists press the argument that unequal social and economic conditions suppress and distort our essentially "good nature". Meanwhile, however, extensive human pathology or collective moral failure seems all too recalcitrant. At the personal level, simply stop and consider how difficult most of us find it to change habits that are detrimental to our health and relationships. Where does such weakness of will come from? Are we just wilfully self-defeating, responsible for all our own failures (including backache) or are we riddled with foundational flaws of which we are usually ignorant?

Let's now look at the nuanced meanings of failure. Obviously it refers to some sort of breakdown, some malfunctioning or underperformance. A little less obviously, it logically implies antecedent non-failure: all was apparently running smoothly or looking perfect, as expected, before this negative event. It is as if we hold a belief, perhaps a fantasy, that things should always function without fail. Life *should* be just, beautiful, flawless; or if it is not so, then it surely *must* become so following our heroic efforts to make it so. We know very well this is not and cannot be the case (and might well turn dystopian in the event of an overdose of perfection) but something within us is offended or disappointed; we feel let down when our expectations are ruptured. In the schema offered here, however, failure in different degrees is ever present.

As an example of a philosophical attempt to lay the groundwork for an understanding of mental illness, the philosopher George Graham asks if the following statement is true or satisfactory: "A mental disorder should be analyzed as the harmful failure of a mental faculty to function as nature designed. Something is a

mental disorder if and only if it is a harmful mental dysfunction"
(2010: 21).

Graham decides that this will not do because blindness, for
example, is partly a mental phenomenon. Even in this small vignette
of attempted analysis we can see how much (dysfunctional?) effort
goes into trying to clarify something that most of us apprehend
intuitively or by common sense: that some individuals suffer terribly
from a disturbance of what we regard as "normal" mental functioning. We haggle over names and related ethics, and we search for
remedies, but we already *know* that something is not right and that
it entails suffering. Also in this small passage above we see that the
terms "disorder", "failure" and "dysfunction" are used very similarly,
almost tautologically. It is as if Graham, the author, or any one of
us can axiomatically stand outside of mental illness and pronounce
on it with precision and detachment. But we do not ask, perhaps
we *never* seriously ask, if our species itself is mentally disturbed
and our primary tool of analysis, language, isn't somewhat dysfunctional. Indeed, I am partly asking in this book whether all human
beings suffer from a form of "pathology" that we have deceived
ourselves into considering normal. As I suggest below with reference to Walter Benjamin, language is replete with duplications and
ambiguities; in other words, to some extent it fails us and our need
to communicate clearly.

Our topic contains many related "f" words: failure, fail, failing,
fallible, fault, flaw, fall, fiasco, fracas, flop, flunk, fuck-up, falter. It
embraces a wide scale and many moral and aesthetic dimensions:
defect, imperfection, peccadillo, error, breakdown, malfunction,
collapse, catastrophe, meltdown, sin, blunder, blemish, pathology,
foolishness, folly, wrong, abortion, underperformance, inferiority.
We might add the terms lack, disappoint, mistake, defeat, let down,
end, shortcoming, miss, frailty, fragility, weakness, misjudge. Again,
we may be tempted to believe or be lulled into thinking that these
all represent quite distinct phenomena; indeed, they do to some

extent belong to different contexts and have different uses. But they are joined by the sense of things going wrong, not meeting our expectations, being less than the ideal. Failure and the fear of failure lie at the centre of a web of risk, fallibility, adversity, stigma and disappointment that none of us can escape.

I turn now to some distinctly different kinds of failure. Some of these come from within or surround us, and others precede us. Let me suggest that, first, we have a kind of failure of constancy. As already discussed, human beings seem to expect or fantasize an existence of untroubled continuity – for the sun to rise, food to be available, loved ones to be safe, life to be fair, and so on – but we all know that things go wrong in nature: that both large-scale catastrophes will happen and smaller-scale, personal misfortunes will interrupt our sense of continuity. Apparently we are so dependent on non-shocking conditions, on an "average expectable environment", that many of us experience very problematic states of post-traumatic stress disorder, with neurological features, when exposed to life-threatening shocks.

We are all subject to biological failure. We can and we do use every possible euphemism to avoid the unpleasant subject of death. But some pregnancies do not even become viable biologically; some babies are born and live with terrible genetic faults, visible and invisible, that cannot be escaped and that may severely limit their life chances. One interpretation of biological failure is that not succeeding to reproduce is the only failure. All of us, as "soft machines", are susceptible to accidents and diseases. Many live in pain. And all of us must die of one form of biological failure or another. It is clear why Schopenhauer was sympathetic to Buddhism with its identification of suffering as central in human life.

Since we are highly dependent on tools, technology and every kind of mechanical aid for our standard and style of living, mechanical failure has become a serious interruption to our sense of mastery and our comfort. Everything from collapsing bridges, inadequate water barriers, faulty brakes, aeroplane faults and the compromised safety of nuclear power plants to medical errors, internet failures and serious glitches in military hardware can bring unexpected deaths and arrested daily functioning to our complex, technically dependent lives. The Northeast blackout of 2003, for example, affected the lives of around five million people in Canada and the USA. High temperatures and other chance and unforeseen factors combined to create a power surge that led to huge electrical failure affecting transport, water supplies, communication and industry. Our mechanical and technological environment is progressively internalized, so that we may now feel helpless and lost when our computer or smartphone breaks down.

Failures in intergroup, social and interpersonal cohesion create mayhem and heartache for human beings. On the one hand we have the gifts of rationality, communication and cooperation (underpinned by a great deal of religion and philosophy) but on the other we have disproportionate aggression, anxious territoriality, a readiness to engage in war and the weapons of mass destruction to wipe us all out. While failures in romantic, sexual, marital and family relationships are not usually fatal, they frequently cause acute heartache, hardships and long-term negative consequences, and do include some cases of murder and suicide. Our empathic failings are pervasive.

Moral failures are abundant and seen in apparently universal *akrasia*, or weakness of will, but also in conative failure. As Edmund Burke allegedly said, "All that is necessary for the triumph of evil is that good men do nothing". The strong argument here is that all human beings are failures morally since we all acquiesce in a civilization of much selfishness, greed, mendacity and violence. Some of us stand up for selective good causes (usually those with which we identify personally) to some extent but most of us opt for an easy life of compromise. It is difficult to say whether our common habit of denying how bad matters are is a question of false consciousness (we can no longer see the extent of tragedy and absurdity around us) or of moral failure, of our seeing but doing nothing. Moral failures, like sins of commission or omission, occur at both individual and collective levels.

Aesthetic failure is that domain of life in which ugliness prevails or in which our best efforts to produce beauty result in imperfection. We may have relatively little choice about our own physical characteristics until genetic engineering and cosmetic surgery become commonplace and cheap. We say someone's face is her fortune and another's face doesn't fit. The French novelist Michel Houellebecq, celebrated and hated for his bitter Schopenhauerian negativity, declared in *Whatever* that "sexuality is a system of social hierarchy"; to a great extent we are driven by sex, and sexual selection favours the beautiful over the ugly. And in spite of our best architectural designs and aspirations, vulgarity, ugliness and urban decay seem commonplace. A clear example of this is overcrowded cityscapes and slums, alongside the rape of forests and green areas. We do not seem much to notice or mind or, if we do, we feel powerless to change matters. In a different vein, we may refer to an eccentric piece of architecture as a folly, recognizing its aesthetic failings with fondness or amusement. It is also problematic to note that youth is typically beautiful compared with old age. Many philosophers have tackled aesthetics but it may be that in mathematics we see the supreme hope of attaining perfection, of formulae that cannot fail.

Then we have epistemological failure and cognitive errors. The very existence of philosophy attests to the problems of non-consensual and non-axiomatic knowledge. While science now at least aims at the discovery of incontrovertible truths, human history is littered with myths, legends and all manner of disputed and frequently aggression-arousing claims to knowledge and counter-knowledge. At the individual level, cognitive errors abound in our lack of logic, making faulty inferences, being influenced by superstition and so on. Etymology of the terms "crazy" and "cracked" suggests pervasive mental flaws that we might liken to geological faults. If you are not a good knowledge processor you may be labelled or feel stupid. If we pause to consider catastrophic failures of human judgement, the case of the *Titanic* immediately comes to mind. *Human error* lies behind tragic medical misdiagnoses, many plane crashes and a wide range of other troubling phenomena.

To this list we should add the failure of meaning or purpose of life. This failure is probably at its most acute in our own time and perhaps coincides with the so-called death of God. Often associated with Nietzsche and nihilism, the death of belief in God should be seen in the light of the eighteenth-century Enlightenment and the rise of science and intellectual critique, later from Karl Marx, Charles Darwin and Sigmund Freud. A great deal of twentieth-century literature also conveys a sense of the meaninglessness, anomie and absurdity of life, unsurprisingly in times of world wars, the Holocaust and increasing urbanization, boredom, loneliness and dehumanizing work routines. A major paradox at the heart of this failure is that the more we have, the less we seem to appreciate life.

It is inevitable and valid that the question must arise, simply because all the negative events above can attract the term "failure": is there any logical or justified convergence in a unitary concept of failure, such as the one presented in this book? Well, we certainly have an outstanding precedent for such an overarching concept in the Abrahamic religions' theology of the Fall. Since disobeying God's original commandment, we have brought all kinds of "failure" (understood as sin) on ourselves and on the world we live in, according to this view. The concept of original sin was promoted by Augustine in the fourth century and by Aquinas in the thirteenth. Michael Moriarty (2006) pushes an argument that it was further raised in seventeenth-century France by René Descartes, Nicolas

Malebranche, Blaise Pascal and Jean-François Senault. Among some later theologians the concept of original sin is widely disliked and dismissed, however, both among atheists and many Christians, for its negative, stigmatizing and guilt-inducing properties. Alan Jacobs (2008) acknowledges that it has been called "baleful, repulsive and revolting".

In its simplest form, original sin suggests that God's creation was wholly good (flawless, perfect, not subject to failure or death) but human beings spoiled this ideal scenario through their wilful sin, corruption and vice. Original sin, ushered in by Adam and Eve and subsequently passed down through the generations, is therefore anthropogenic sin and can be reversed only by Jesus Christ and belief in him (with obvious variations in other religions). Without religious salvation, such arguments run, we continue to sin individually and cast sinful conditions all around us that will eventually result in the catastrophe of Armageddon.

This concept of original, global sin is hard to bear, since it suggests that everything we touch goes wrong. As Stephen Mulhall puts it, "Human beings are not only naturally capable of acting – even perhaps disposed to act – sinfully, but are always already turned against themselves, against the true and against the good, by virtue of their very condition as human" (2005: 6).

Sin of such negative magnitude and intergenerational heaviness is in our very nature and we are helpless to pull ourselves out of it, and yet we also have the theological tradition that imputes agency to each of us. As we see in the seven deadly sins of sloth, pride, envy, covetousness, lust, gluttony and wrath, such sins or vices are construed as particular forms of personal, moral failure. Any of us might be capable of not sinning or sinning less: of improving our behaviour, regardless of collective human tendencies to original sin. In pre-psychological or pre-psychoanalytic understanding, failures to act with due energy, humility, appreciation, contentment, chastity, gastronomic restraint and placidity are nevertheless correctable. The philosopher Gabriele Taylor (2006) discusses the importance of such "countervailing virtues" in her analysis of the well-known "ordinary vices".

It is important here to recall that in its Greek sense of *hamartia*, from Socrates and Aristotle, sin means "missing the mark". It also has connotations of error of judgement, mistake, accident, moral deficit and character flaw. For Aristotle it included the concept of a "tragic flaw". Interestingly, this sense of deviating from a moral or behavioural norm does not quite carry forwards today in the domains of crime and mental illness. We do not today generally refer to a criminal as a sinner or failure but think of him or her as one who has knowingly or pathologically broken the law, who has perhaps taken a risk but did not get away with it. Similarly, the person suffering from some form of severe mental illness is not generally referred to as a failure but as unfortunate.

We do not speak of Hitler as a failure (unless as a failed painter and military tactician) but as an evil perpetrator of genocide. We do not describe the perpetrators of 9/11 as moral failures but as evil, callous, psychopathic and so on (although we might well claim their theology to be seriously flawed but, perhaps somewhat reluctantly, we cannot fault their planning or courage). My point here is simply that the nuances of our terminology are problematic and trends in moral perception change over time. But we seem emotionally attached to particular words and we may mistakenly attribute greater significance to them than is due. In all the cases mentioned above, can we not provisionally agree that something is awry or amiss, is off the mark, or has failed?

Today the concept of sin has relatively little of its former currency, or so it may seem. One of our many human problems is the complexity and distortion of language; linked with this is our obstinately tribal nature, which permeates not only territorial identities but also intellectual traditions and divisions between them. In other words, philosophers, theologians, psychologists, sociologists and others constantly criticize each other's theories and create new theories that ostensibly set out to correct the failings of previous theories and lead to greater clarity, truth, social utility and so on. Socrates, Plato and Aristotle addressed moral problems in Greece, the Buddha in Nepal, Jesus in Israel, Mohammed in Mecca, all within many centuries of each other but in different locations, all leaving distinct legacies. On one reading of these traditions, they were all seeking solutions to universal, painful human problems of identity, morality, meaning, death and salvation, and perhaps, in some cases, intellectual clarity. But we have to ask whether they have (i) failed to promote any convergence of enquiry, or consensus, and (ii) ultimately failed altogether to have a significant moral and practical impact on human affairs. It was the repeated lament of the Indian philosopher Krishnamurti that this was indeed the case, echoing the early search of the Buddha, who consulted and researched among the sages and teachers of his time to no avail.

The mid-eighteenth century saw the Enlightenment in Europe propel the cause of reason in philosophy and science, leading to a major surge in scepticism towards religious traditions and a massive growth of technology and industry, and social sciences. The moral philosopher Alasdair MacIntyre has been famously critical of the Enlightenment Project, arguing that it "had to fail" and has indeed failed, largely because it attempted to ignore or bypass the virtue ethics of Aristotle, later refined by Aquinas and still the strongest candidate for an adequate moral theory in the view of MacIntyre (2007). For the vast majority of humanity such arguments probably have little direct relevance to their everyday lives, in spite of the value of MacIntyre's critique of emotivism, managerialism and other contemporary ethical systems, and of the principle that we are all free rational agents. MacIntyre is highly critical of existentialism, consigning Jean-Paul Sartre for example to the category of mere "emotivist rhetoric".

Whether consciously incorporating religious themes and terminology, rejecting them or unwittingly duplicating them, many philosophers address these questions in one form of jargon or another. Martin Heidegger did not explicitly draw on Christian theology but his concept of fallenness (or "falling prey to", in some translations) raises the central theme of inauthenticity in human behaviour: we are aware of this fallenness but compelled to suppress our awareness. Existentialist thinkers generally make abundant use of a dichotomy between being and non-being, real and false self, and in the concepts of alienation or estrangement emphasize our being sundered from another, original, better or potential state of consciousness. This dualism has seemed inescapable in most philosophical and theological systems, unless we credit postmodernist thinkers with taking us into acceptable intellectual pluralism and diversity. Splitting, disagreeing and fragmenting is the overall trend, perhaps representing the disordered complexity of entropy.

Sartre's well-known arguments revolving around being and non-being include looking at the problem of whether we can speak meaningfully of non-being at all. But we can easily say that once I did not exist (although being itself always did) and one day I shall cease to be. As this entity, after the process of what Schopenhauer called the dissolution of all our parts, I will *not be*. More helpful to our discussion is to point out that any particular form of being is subject to change, the vitality and viability of each of us being susceptible to corrosion by flaws and failure events. Aristotle wrote in terms of generation and corruption, or coming to be and passing away, and how these may differ, or not, from mere alteration. I may seem a pale version of my former self following some traumatic event from which I cannot bounce back, or existentially choose not to recover well from. Human being especially is subject to a chronic inward negation, which Sartre refers to as bad faith:

One puts oneself in bad faith as one goes to sleep and one is in bad faith as one dreams. Once this mode of being has been realized, it is as difficult to get out of it as to wake oneself up; bad faith is a type of being in the world, like waking or dreaming, which by itself tends to perpetuate itself.   (Sartre 1958: 68)

Most of us appear to choose to be less than we can be. We opt for a partly inauthentic existence. However hard it is to shake ourselves out of bad faith, as Sartre admits, the choice remains. This position, developed from Søren Kierkegaard's "sickness unto death" and Heidegger's fallenness, leaves us with access to full being, whatever interpretation we settle on. We could say that we let ourselves down or fail ourselves. We might agree that we share some human state of fallenness or bad faith but always individually remain free, as Sartre insisted. Authentic existence is a tough demand for most of us, since the exercise of perpetual free choice, constantly waking oneself up, in a trance-like anti-authentic world, can feel like too heroic a challenge.

As I have argued, philosophers and theologians, for all the subtlety of their thinking, seem unable or disinclined to agree on much or conclude anything. While this can be accepted as inevitably slow scholarly work in progress, it can also be criticized as being off the mark: failing to comprehend the seriousness of the human condition (fiddling while Rome burns). Sometimes known as the love of wisdom, philosophy can be characterized as a love of, or even obsession with, sophistry and argument: perhaps "philosophistry". Indeed, in different ways Lee McIntyre (2006) complains of a "resistance to knowledge" and Nicholas Maxwell (2007) of a continuing serious failure among scholars to address our species' need for wisdom, which has both perennial and urgent aspects. Heidegger regarded himself as taking human fallenness unusually seriously but one fellow philosopher dismisses his work as "huge masses of hideous gibberish" (Paul Edwards, in Hendricks 2004: 38).

Failure may be understood in the following way. First we have the so-called second law of thermodynamics, or entropy, which ultimately means that everything that is in a certain form in a closed system *must* one day start to become over-complex, somewhat disordered, then irreversibly damaged, and finally cease to exist. Entropy is pervasive and runs through all phenomena, from human beings themselves to buildings, cities and planets. As many ancient Greek philosophers (famously Heraclitus) noted, change is universal and purity tends to become impure, or one becomes many, as in Plotinus' concept of tolmatic inevitability. Humans are ambivalent about change: it is both inevitable and sometimes releasing and exciting, and also threatening and unwelcome to our psychological need for constancy.

This is linked with the principle of fallibility: the unavoidable observation that anything that exists has the potential to fail, either in its functioning or in its very being. Any romantic relationship or business project can fail. Fallibility is entwined with viability, and we might loosely refer to these two as death and life trends respectively, or as the poles of imperfection and perfection.

Let us also note a phenomenon we can refer to as a faultline or flaw. One of the most dramatic and well known of these is the geological faultline leading to earthquakes. It has been speculated that epileptic seizures may have features in common with earthquake activity. But a "basic fault" of a psychological nature is observed in some human beings too, and tragedy is usually the outcome of an existing fault, or serious flaw.

We then have failures as marked events and we might see these as manifestations of underlying faults. Our hidden flaws are sure to result in small cracks, then larger cracks, and sometimes even catastrophic disasters. Failures may be somewhat predictable, or not. They may be periodic or they may come in clusters or very infrequently and in random distributions. The Japanese earthquake of early 2011 was followed by a devastating tsunami resulting in thousands of human deaths, and subsequently by breakdowns in the security of some nuclear facilities, threatening more lives, all alongside a growing precariousness in Japanese economics. Within a human life some of us experience clusters of ill health, relationship failure and job insecurity in a short space of time. We speak of fatal flaws, we say the rot has set in, someone is on the road to ruin.

Recalling the notion of moral failure, we note that we all have seemingly inevitable "failings", flaws in our personality, little vices and peccadilloes, tiny mood shifts within neurotic rhythms. These may be non-threatening and even charming quirks – we may like eccentrics or admire slightly flawed buildings – but little cracks in a bridge may be signs of worse to come, "accidents waiting to happen" (Petroski 1992). Near misses, events that, owing to luck, didn't quite become failures or even catastrophes, perhaps also belong here.

In spite of the prevalence of failure, we seem to have no philosophy of failure as such. Acknowledging and lamenting this, Joel Fisher (2010) quite light-heartedly suggests creating a discipline of *anaprokopology* or the study of "not success" (although the translation from the Greek is botched and *hamartiology* might be better). My own not-yet-successful attempt to establish the study of *anthropathology* or human sickness works along partly similar lines (Feltham 2007). But even without such a focus we do have perennial themes of mismatches occurring in nature and human affairs that cannot be ignored. Life as given is not perfectly comprehensible, satisfying or just but must be constantly worked at philosophically, politically and personally. Existence as given lacks something and our efforts never completely fill this lack. Early philosophy was partly science in the making (understanding the natural world outside us) but also always significantly about human perception and conduct. We certainly have themes of appearance and reality, and the failure of a clear match or accessible match between them (Plato); of life as suffering and failing to produce a satisfactory solution (Schopenhauer); understanding as

29

always limited or defective, causing alienation (Hegel, Heidegger); the notion of humanity as "crooked timber" or a "bent twig" from Kant, later borrowed by Isaiah Berlin to argue for inevitable cultural pluralism and anti-utopianism, and expanded on pessimistically by John Gray (2002).

It is not entirely true to say that we have no philosophy of failure. Paul Ricoeur, in his *Fallible Man* (1986), presents a case for the human species ("man" in his day) being susceptible to fault (like geological faults), *faille* (break, breach), *écart* (gap or digression), *fêlure* (rift) and other terms suggesting error and aberrance. Ricoeur calls on Descartes' view that we are "subject to an infinity of errors" and an "infinity of imperfections" and on Pascal's account of us as "full of faults". Affective fragility, misery, moral weakness, fallibility as opening the possibility of evil, are all concepts dwelled upon by Ricoeur.

An unavoidable obstacle in human endeavours is the ambiguity of language. Consider these phrases: (at an airport) "failure to comply with these regulations may result in baggage being confiscated or destroyed" and (in debate on the moral philosophy of justice and equal social contributions) "failure to pull your weight". Are these truly examples of failure? We could substitute a more common negative term with no loss of meaning: "not complying with" or "not pulling your weight". This illustrates only one language problem: that of different terms meaning the same or similar things, creating potential confusion. But our Babelian inheritance also contains problems of national conflicts; abstract and symbolic language that gets confused with reality and can lead to religious conflict; language that obscures or is misleading; language that is or can be deliberately deceptive. Unfortunately, academic philosophy and many other academic discourses are frequently unenlightening for the majority of people. We might simply say that language, or languages, alongside their advantages, have commonly failed to mirror or clarify reality and have often made matters worse.

Benjamin referred to the "prattle" of language, indeed of an "abyss of prattle", "fallen tongues" and "overnaming". "Having too many names is worse than having none" (Pensky 2001: 53). Ludwig Wittgenstein quite bluntly stated that "A main source of our failure to understand is that we do not command a clear view of the use of our words" (1967: 122). Philosophies of linguistic analysis and formal logic separate phenomena for study, while philosophies concerned with the big questions of existence, of ontology, seek broad underlying patterns. In this book I am seeking and often assuming such underlying patterns and explanations. Clearly we have "something rather than nothing" in cosmic and human existence but we cannot get away from the persistence of "non-being", most obviously in distortion, decay and death. For me, these phenomena are virtually synonymous with flaws, faults, failings, sins, errors, failure and the ultimate failure: our personal deaths and the death of the universe. It is a consolation to discover that there are flaws and systemic failures that pervade all phenomena, including my own life.

2. Failure across the lifespan

The typical human lifespan may be said to run from the moment of birth to the moment of death. Indeed, T. S. Eliot summarized existence as "birth, copulation and death" and some philosophers treat childhood and old age as states that are peripheral to the project of adult rationality, with "philosophy of childhood" being a very late development in the discipline.

Millions of sperm compete to fertilize one egg: it seems that the vast majority *must* fail, that competition and failure are prerequisites for "fitness". Something obviously begins at conception, although it is reckoned that as many as 75 per cent of conceptions technically miscarry. Stillbirths, defects caused by intrauterine factors, diseases, birth complications and negative genetic factors, and infant deaths all attest to the human susceptibility to the earliest faults in development. Up to one in five premature babies are killed by just one bowel disease, for example: necrotizing enterocolitis. Dante Cicchetti and Elaime F. Walker (2003) discuss "aberrant neurodevelopment" in relation to schizophrenia, autism, substance abuse, personality disorders and depression, among other conditions. "Failure to thrive" (or not growing and gaining due weight) is well documented. The potential for fallibility and actual failures and flaws is present from the outset, if we allow ourselves to speak broadly of biological and systemic failures. Roberts (2011) embraces this "embodiment-as-error" as part of his discussion of pervasive errors in human enterprises.

The long gestation period for human pregnancy makes for some vulnerabilities in the foetus. Things can go wrong at any stage. Intrauterine damage is a topic that is partly well documented and partly only speculative. Likewise, birth complications and birth trauma are areas in which consensus is far from complete. Radical obstetricians such as Frederick Leboyer and Michel Odent have complained about traditional flawed medical practices that not only let mothers and their babies down but traumatize them. But enough accounts exist of long labours (painful for both mother and baby), oxygen starvation, strangulation by the chord, harsh medical deliveries and unnecessary Caesareans for us to have to reckon with birth as a precarious and fallible process. There is a theory that some of us are born with an optimal sense of "birthing ourselves" successfully, while others are born rather passively and experience all life thereafter as a somewhat pointless struggle at best (i.e. the sense of failure and doom is inborn). Such ideas do not sit well with the *tabula rasa* views of philosophers such as John Locke and defenders of free will. Some of us will be born with visible "birth defects", minor or major, that shape our fortune, and some will have "faulty genes" that may be switched on at various points in our lives to dramatic effect, sometimes bringing into our lives tragic disabilities and/or causing premature deaths. This is complicated territory since genetic defects have long caused human suffering, medical progress has eliminated or reduced much of this suffering, yet equally we may inadvertently create new problems via our new technologies and ways of life. Human existence doesn't necessarily proceed in a one-way, improvement-only direction.

Crucial bonding between mother and baby can fail. Postnatal depression and postnatal psychosis, occurring in a significant minority of mothers, can lead to later serious developmental failures in children. A single case proves nothing, of course, but a friend tells me he is convinced his mother's postnatal depression set him up for later failure at school, his own depression, failed marriage, occupational underperformance and even failing his driving test eight times. Whether or not his attribution of the main determinant of his failures is correct, this case reminds us that we seem always to crave explanations, often to soothe or excuse ourselves, and these explanations are often false or unhelpful. Interestingly, Robert Rowland Smith's popular philosophy text *Driving with Plato: The Meaning of Life's Milestones* (2011) includes a chapter on "passing your driving test" that omits any Platonic guidance, and fails to mention *failing* your driving test, as if passing is something of an automatic rite of passage to inevitable self-realization. Failing your driving test is not merely a delay in driving alone and feeling like an adult but for some a (usually short-term) devastating comment on self-worth or, for young men, "manhood". Anyway, the *possibility* exists in this example that an early negative event leads towards significant later failures.

In some religious accounts each of us exists across many incarnations before and after this present lifetime, depending on unique karmic factors. I shall concentrate here mainly on the single lifetime. Individual human development is also usually portrayed in conventional linear developmental terms as successful progress from one milestone or maturational task to another. Psychologists mainly rule this roost but psychotherapists, novelists and biographers also contribute abundantly. Less well known, perhaps, are the contributions of philosophers.

I quoted from Schopenhauer in the previous chapter. That this view is 150 years old, that Schopenhauer is thought by most to be terribly misanthropic, and that this is a rather male view, we must acknowledge. But even Schopenhauer allows for a happy childhood and exultant youth that many modern psychoanalytic accounts dismiss. Sartre famously declared that he had loathed his childhood but he did not blame it for any lack of freedom. Recall that some Christian theology describes us as born in sin, with Eve bound to suffer in childbirth and Adam destined for painful lifelong toil. We could easily put such narrative in positive terms: we begin in the joy of love, flourish as innocent children and healthy adolescents, enjoy happy careers and relationships, and live long lives supported by excellent medical care. Neither is an objective account, nor do many of us lead typical lives. Some of us are luckier, happier, healthier and wealthier than others. Some of us are hardier, more resilient by temperament. Very often those born well, into lucky circumstances, with lucky genes, thrive far better, giving the lie to virtue-based and merit-oriented philosophies of success. And whatever we think about our lives and however cleverly we contrive to avoid accidents, illnesses and misfortunes, many of us experience misfortunes and we must all die within a few decades. David Shields (2008), not an obvious misanthrope like Schopenhauer, nevertheless portrays the life course as studded with decline, as the very title of his book *The Thing About Life Is That One Day You'll Be Dead* shows.

We cannot ask to be born but once alive relatively few of us want to die or suffer, but we all do. David Benatar (2006), among other moral philosophers, examines the pros and cons of human existence. Concluding that pain outweighs pleasure, he does not recommend suicide but does suggest that it would be better to decide not to have children, since to do so is inevitably to bring suffering into the world with them. Cioran, the celebratedly arch-pessimistic Romanian aphorist, similarly decried human existence in *The Trouble with Being Born*. When he says "Whether one succeeds or not comes down to the same thing" (Cioran 1998: 63), he means that life is ultimately absurd and disappointing whatever happens within it in detail.

At the beginning, we are vulnerable babies and infants, a key feature of young human beings being our complete dependency on adult caretakers for sustenance and stability. This is familiar territory for psychoanalysts and psychotherapists. Our adult caretakers are fallible, they may be poor parents, they may themselves have had inadequate parenting, they may even be abusive and sadistic. Not forgetting the majority who probably do their best, and acknowledging controversies about all this, we must reckon with the unfortunate likelihood that sometimes "They fuck you up, your mum and dad", as the poet Philip Larkin put it so memorably. They let you down, they fail you. They can all too easily err on the side of either harsh discipline or indulgence, as if any parenting strategy may backfire. "But they were fucked up in their turn" reminds us of the transgenerational failure process, which "deepens like a coastal shelf" (another interesting geological metaphor). If these failings are bad enough, we may develop what some therapists refer to as a "basic fault" in the structure of the personality, resulting in lifelong maladjustment.

All such early developmental failures may lead to what Freud called "hysterical misery", to be distinguished from the "common unhappiness" that most of us experience. Optimists of various radical, liberal and romantic hues will protest that things don't happen this way, or if they do they are readily reversed by better social conditions, by therapy, by self-determination, or by love. Radical pessimists will perhaps say that this isn't putting the case strongly enough: millennia of genetic, evolutionary, generationally cumulative traumas and current patriarchal and capitalist conditions conspire to ensure that our species flaws remain undisturbed, indeed are endlessly compounded. "Man hands on misery to man", in Larkin's terms, but in an even stronger argument for anthropathology we might say that our species flaws are actively reproduced and deepened, and our typical analyses are superficial and erroneous.

Our vulnerability as babies and infants usually elicits caring attitudes and behaviours from others but some young humans are badly let down by parents, step-parents and other carers. A significant minority are seriously neglected, sometimes to the point of death, sometimes by inadequate young parents who were poorly parented themselves. I still recall working many years ago with one young couple with criminal convictions resulting from putting their baby in a cardboard box to stop it crying, a desperate and stupid act ending in the neglected baby's death. Add to such gross neglect the catalogue of physical and sexual abuses that even many very young children are subjected to, and we must realize how fallible and fragile human parenting can be and how severely damaged the most vulnerable can be. Indeed, realizing that these abuses do occur, we appoint social workers to monitor problem families. When neglectful or abusive parents visit their own failings and hatreds on children, social workers sometimes fail to spot the abuses and are then themselves blamed for failing to do so. Meanwhile many of these children grow up traumatized and fail to develop "normally", some of them going on under pressure from dark inner forces to become abusers themselves. When working for some years in a probation hostel I got to know many young adults who had progressed from highly faulty parenting to foster parents and children's homes only to fail to thrive or gain any purchase on "normal" successful relationships, home life and jobs, ending up in prisons with repeated criminal convictions. An unpalatable hypothesis here is that early failures outside of our individual control are often compounded throughout life.

After and alongside our viable or non-viable period of intense parenting most of us compulsorily attend school. If lucky we may have experienced unconditional love and nurturant individual attention at home. Most schools are tacitly structured around principles of group conformity, obedience, sedentariness and competition. School is where many of us have learned where we sit in the social pecking order. In some cases young people learn early on that they are academic failures and carry this stigma through their whole lives. School is one arena where we are often assessed according to annual performances in tests and examinations. Low marks, the very term "fail" or euphemisms such as "requires attention" or "needs to work harder" can determine your subjective sense of self and also your life chances.

Another friend tells me that as an infant he was off school sick for a few days. After he returned he could no longer keep up with spelling because he'd missed a few key lessons. Thereafter, for decades, he had literacy problems and felt stupid. He felt a failure and blamed this on himself; his whole life was coloured by the experience. Such experiences persist. And this is without the problems of bullying by peers and sometimes teachers. Obviously some young people take to school well and it launches them into successful careers later. That was probably the case for me because I passed a major national exam at age eleven (the 11-plus) and went to grammar school. Although this was a moment of success in itself (I was a winner, I was rewarded with presents), it had its downside. As a shy, working-class boy among eight hundred mainly middle-class boys, I struggled. I did very well in some subjects but failed spectacularly at others. Science and sports were a nightmare for me, and an all-male environment hardly succeeded in sensitizing me to the female world. My mother was not a good mother and my education probably exacerbated my inadequacies in male–female relationships. By the age of eighteen I was an anguished young man and could manage to pass only one of my A-level exams, and I left school ill equipped for any career. Should the failure involved be laid at my own, my parents' or the school's doorstep? Or possibly at all these, as a compound failure of the kind so common among human beings? Could we not devise, if we so wished, an educational system not constructed around the defining poles of success and failure?

Most of my working-class peers went to "secondary modern school" and internalized the message that they were second-rate people. In her *Educational Failure and Working Class White Children in Britain*, Gillian Evans (2006) exposes the ways in which schools themselves similarly fail some of their pupils. Some proportion of young people will do worse than others in any competitive educational system. Perhaps it is part of the tragedy of humanity that we must always choose and our choices are fallible, whether as individuals or as social and educational policy-makers. Is it better to create elitist schools or a comprehensive school system? Is mass education the only economically viable option or do small schools offer better attention and pastoral care? For anarchists, compulsory education fails to respect human rights altogether. For some observers it may seem that an exclusive and expensive education is necessarily flawed in terms of social justice, not to mention its detrimental effects on emotional maturity, the failings of many public schoolboys having been well noted. Or we might suggest that for many the impact of education is minimal. Some of my early peers who failed their 11-plus went on to make much more successful careers and more money than I ever did.

Compulsory education is said to prepare us for later life, mainly for work. As many critics of education have pointed out, it rarely, if ever, helps us to understand matters of intimate relationships, alongside work a "cornerstone of our humanness", according to Freud. School rarely helps us with the most practical of matters we face later, such as personal finances, diet and health, how to vote, how to understand ourselves and overcome personal problems, and so on. Instead it usually consists of a few traditional subjects that may be of no use or stimulation to most (physics, geography), perhaps with some fashionable or politically expedient subjects such as citizenship. Mass education decided and imposed from above must commonly fail a large number of unconsulted students who spend years enduring it and have little to show for it. The very assumption that the most intensive education should come early on in one's life may yet prove to be erroneous, especially with the prospect of ever-increasing longevity. Childhood education is one area in which some philosophers have sharply disagreed, Jean-Jacques Rousseau, for example, finding absurd Locke's insistence on reasoning, on training children for adulthood, instead of honouring their age-related interests and needs.

With adolescence come physiological changes, sexual desires and social pressures. We might say that the mismatch between biology and society is irresolvable. It is a cliché to claim that at puberty young people are capable of sexual arousal and activity but that they are emotionally immature. Social and religious policies attempt to steer young people away from sex that could result in pregnancies inconvenient to their educational stage and economic capacity, and from problems of premature commitment and sexual infections. But the tensions between powerful sexual desires and often rather dull educational and career paths cannot be easily dispelled. Biology makes us sexual years before we may be deemed ready for, or wise enough to engage in, the parenting that attends pregnancy and childbirth: a tragic mismatch if ever there was one. In this sense accessible and non-stigmatic contraception may be considered a successful solution to this mismatch.

Teenagers also commonly experience a maelstrom of anguish, boredom, risk-taking, questioning of adult conventions, confusion and ambivalence about sexuality and social roles, and an array of hormonal disturbances. Acne and menstruation are just two of the blessings of this stage of life. Many first experience sex as a fumbling, unsatisfactory business attended by anxieties about attractiveness, premature ejaculation, orgasmic targets, performance and love. Many of us have by this time been diagnosed with eye problems and some of us are becoming obese or anorexic, or tall and gangly, or have remained unattractively short. Very often society finds adolescents difficult to deal with and has no satisfactory provision for them. It is not surprising, then, that this is a time when some go off the rails into addiction and crime and some experience the onset of mental illnesses. Jean Piaget has it that this is the time when the formal operations stage kicks in and adolescents can reason abstractly. But clearly some are able thus to reason, or interested in doing so, more than others and it is unclear at what point we can consider ourselves truly existentially free.

Lives are measured in milestones and failure to reach these in a timely fashion is a common cause of anxiety and judgement. Coupling is expected from adolescence onwards, and committed dyadic relationships are usually expected by the twenties or thirties, so that failure to secure such status by then implies an important failed milestone. There is (considered to be) something seriously wrong with you if you're a forty-year-old virgin, for example, even if asexuality is thought to describe about 1 per cent of the population. Some people fail to get much romantic or sexual interest and may be regarded as being "on the shelf", left unwanted, distinctly failures in love. Critics of philosophy sometimes allege that a disproportionate number of philosophers are ivory tower bachelors but the sex lives of Foucault, Bertrand Russell and Sartre flatly contradict this view.

In the world of heterosexual coupledom, living together for some years usually implies a run-up to having children. It probably remains the case that most women who declare they don't want children are regarded with ongoing sexism as a bit odd. It is reckoned that worldwide one in seven couples experience difficulties conceiving, which frequently leads to distress. This failure to conceive may be rectified but is often accompanied by the belief that "I'm not a proper woman, or man". Whether childlessness is chosen or biologically dictated, religious attitudes have strongly underpinned the belief that coupling serves a procreative imperative and childlessness signifies a problematic state. Or one may be a priest, monk or nun, or avowedly child-free existentialist (like Cioran, Kierkegaard, Nietzsche, Sartre *et al.*) or a moral philosopher like David Benatar, who has explicit moral grounds for not bringing children into this world. Hegel's view, however, was that the full family life was superior to that of childlessness.

But having children is not automatically a condition of fulfilment. However delightful, babies can also bring many challenges to couples and growing children generally alter the dynamic of the original couple relationship. Tensions can grow within families, with parents coming to blame themselves ("Where did we go wrong?") for any negative developments. One popular account of a mother's exasperated struggles is provided by Stephanie Calman in *Confessions of a Failed Grown-Up* (2006), the kind of popular text loved for the sense of relief it brings to those who had assumed they were failures as parents. After all, the fairytale expectation many of us inherit is that we will fall in love, stay in love, and have happy, well-adjusted children who will go on to have happy lives themselves. We do not factor in the likelihood that many children will have their failures, will go off the rails or become ill, cause many family conflicts, heartache and sadly, in some cases, die before their parents. This latter scenario is widely recognized as one of life's most tragic failures of expectation.

Similar to the expectation of parenthood is the expectation of a consolidated linear career occurring somewhere between the twenties and forties. At the top end of this expectation sit those who were always meant to, were groomed to, succeed in a prestigious and lucrative career such as law or medicine. Quite early on it becomes obvious if you have failed in this trajectory by not getting into the right university, not getting top grades, not getting the right internship, promotion, salary and so on. Nearer the bottom end, it is still important that you show some ability to stick with an identified career for some years, aimless job-hopping on low wages and periods of unemployment usually signalling a slide into "not amounting to anything" or plain failure. Clearly this judgement is contextual. You may have worked hard but got nowhere, you may have struggled with personal problems, or you may be an entrepreneur whose business ventures have crashed, but the fuzzy nameless representatives of society always seem to be watching and worrying (at least in your head).

I did my share of poorly paid dead-end and temporary jobs in my twenties and thirties – library assistant, kitchen porter, cleaner, residential care worker, administrative assistant – and experienced the frustration, boredom and low self-esteem that usually go with them. I was a drifter who didn't know where he was going, had missed the boat, had no vision or commitment. I was not competitive, I could not buy into the capitalist dream, and I stewed in a mixture of contempt and depression. Although some well-meaning people will tell you that you're doing valuable work, that no one should judge you, that being a good and happy person is more important than climbing a career ladder, you *know* in your heart of hearts that you're being judged, that you've fallen behind, that your chances of success and wealth are getting slimmer by the year. You had your opportunities, you passed some exams, and yet you still blew it. The word "failure" is not required to mark out for you where you stand in the social pecking order. You *know* what a worthless shit you are. Female grace, parenthood and late opportunities saved me from lifelong occupational, status and financial gloom. I even achieved a turnaround in my fortunes. But many do not.

An interesting minority of people opt for a lifestyle that rejects mainstream social values. In this group we can find idiosyncratic rebels like Camus's "outsider" character, anarchists, hippies and others who embrace an alternative lifestyle in the belief that society is the failure, not themselves. Our society does not make space for too many paid thinkers. Or some go through the motions of mainstream citizenship while reserving evenings and weekends for their part-time authentic existence. Much more formally, those choosing to become monks, nuns and celibate priests embody the belief that the standard lifespan expectations regarding ambitions for relationships and careers do not correspond with their personalities or values.

That group of people who used to be labelled "deviants" – criminals, offenders – can be construed as choosing a life of crime and the risks of imprisonment, social stigma and failure status that usually accompanies it. We do not know what proportion of career criminals are successful in amassing wealth and avoiding detection but some proportion of the Mafia, for example, probably fit this profile. This is one of many subcultures that rejects mainstream social values (or some of them) and does its own thing, which leads to greater success than its members might otherwise achieve. But consider the circumstances of the desperate inmate on death row in an American prison. Convicted of armed robbery and murder, he readily assents to the label of "failure" when he says, "Yes, I'm a failure. I knew what I was doing. There's no one to blame but myself." We might accept this at face value but this bid for the dignity of responsibility conceals a childhood filled with abysmal parenting, ubiquitous drug abuse among neighbourhood peers, child abuse and the absence of successful role models. In some circumstances it may be easier to sign up to a belief in (hypothetical) autonomy than to re-experience the terrible emotional pain of having the vulnerable sensitivity of one's formative years crushed. In principle any of us can walk away from an unsuccessful life trajectory. The view is shared by some philosophers and pragmatic American optimists that "you can do and be anything you choose" but is as unrealistic as the belief in total determinism.

On some accounts of lifespan development, we are revisited, perhaps tormented, by those earlier tasks we have failed to achieve. Famously, in middle age we are said commonly to experience midlife crisis. This is a time when men who should know better abruptly leave their wives, become promiscuous, take drugs or drink too much, grow a ponytail, buy a fast car and generally simulate the lifestyle of a hedonistic, affluent twenty- or thirty-something. Middle-aged women are either wiser or more modest, perhaps ending a marriage, taking a younger lover and travelling to exotic places. The concept of the midlife crisis was created by Elliott Jaques in 1965 and perhaps had some credence then; 15 per cent of men are said to have had such experiences. But times and fashions change. Life is more liberal than it was in 1965, people change careers and partners more often, and live longer. A so-called quarter-life crisis has been mooted. As a late developer and a kind of non-conformist, I had no midlife crisis; rather, an ongoing, inner, low-level crisis. I suspect that concepts such as this fail to endure for very long. One can witness people having crises at any age, even if there may be some recognizable characteristics of adults who feel trapped by responsibilities and unfulfilling commitments chosen earlier. Certainly it appears to be common enough for people to spurn long-term commitments when they do not feel pleasurable, which represents a large shift in moral values since the early-to-mid-twentieth century.

What happens very commonly from our teens onwards is that we must recognize some of the choices we may never fulfil if we did not get started early enough and/or had insufficient talent. Many roles in the arts and sports, for example, demand the signs and nurturance of early talent. As we age we are more likely to have to confront the disappointments of unmet dreams and aspirations. You will never become a doctor, an actor, a successful writer, astronaut, scientist and so on unless you are realistically on that trajectory in your earlier decades. This isn't to say these things can *never* happen later in life but they become less and less likely. I was quite a talented artist in my late teens but any prospects of becoming a serious artist are long gone. My wry art teacher chuckled as he wrote the "has a brilliant future behind him" line on my final report. Nor am I at all likely to become the poet or the enlightened Buddha I once dreamt of becoming. Most of us make our own discerning judgements concerning defeatism and optimism, and optimism and realism.

Your strength and co-ordination peak at 19. Your body is the most flexible until age 20; after that, joint function steadily declines. World-class sprinters are almost always in their late teens or early 20s. Your stamina peaks in your late 20s or early 30s; marathon records are invariably held by 25- to 35-year-olds. (Shields 2008: 88)

So-called broken marriages, growing in number, probably reflect more favourable economic circumstances for women, a decline in religious guilt and fear, increasing longevity and other factors. Probably the biggest losers in these circumstances are children. No longer do so many of us stay together "for the sake of the children". There is some evidence that children of divorced parents may later underachieve in school and career and/or go on to experience failed relationships themselves, but it is far from conclusive. Nevertheless, all such observations challenge myths of the happy marriage. Quite apart from those voting with their feet, there are still many who may stay in "committed relationships" out of inertia, fear or guilt, and some who claim to be happily married in order to avoid the unpleasant cognitive dissonance of realizing they no longer love the person they once loved so passionately. There is a finding that the state of "being in love" typically lasts only about eighteen months to three years, after which entropy perhaps begins to eat away at love and partners must be on their guard and work hard to preserve their relationship. While broken marriages once used to be the stigmatic exception, now they are very common, one recent figure for European countries showing ten to sixteen years as the mean length before divorce. This fact must exert an unwelcome pressure of sorts on everyone in a committed relationship: a constant reminder that relational failure is always possible. Love that is romantically based seems not to lend itself to a phlegmatic "Let's see how it goes, it may or may not work" attitude, yet it cannot be blind to the failures of others around it. Erotically based love was seen as a kind of madness by early Greek philosophers, with friendship and other forms of love thought of as probably having more durability.

With some of our achievements behind us, disappointments nearby and limitations in mind, we begin to realize that we are halfway through life, say, and not getting any prettier, cleverer or happier. You're not going to get that big promotion; you have a dauntingly large mortgage; you're never going to go and live in

California. Perhaps you opened that bar in Spain but it didn't work out and the dream is gone. You start wearing glasses, visiting your doctor more often, discover you have high blood pressure. Some fight on in optimism, give up work, sell the house, downsize, go travelling, embrace an exercise programme and complementary medicine. But some of us instinctive Schopenhauerians see these intimations of mortality as the beginning of the end, be that end yet thirty or forty years away. Lifelong routine cosmetic attention, hair dye, botox, hormone replacement therapy, all these to some extent, and increasingly, stave off the reality of ageing and aesthetic failure, but only partly and imperfectly.

For some, life fails to pan out in a way that feels fair. You may work extremely hard in a voluntary organization or in the health sector but have "little to show for it" compared with peers who worked less hard but had better luck or who worked in better remunerated careers such as banking. If you believed what you were told about hard work and honesty, yet witness get-rich-quick chancers flourishing around you while you struggle to make ends meet, a sense of injustice and bitterness might get to you. You may pay great attention to a healthy lifestyle yet succumb to cancer when one or two peers who have led dissolute lives escape such illnesses. You may lead a "blameless life" and yet suffer from redundancy, bankruptcy, divorce, accidents or bereavement. Most us are led to believe in some sort of natural justice based on personal goodness or merit, yet life can prove random in its rewards and adversities. All are susceptible to good and bad moral luck.

In the Judaeo-Christian tradition Job is the exemplar of the stoical and faithful believer in God, refusing, until he finally cracks, to curse God for the great suffering inflicted on him. Anyone can try to follow Job, Epictetus, Boethius, or modern-day cognitive behaviour therapists in accepting their lot uncomplainingly, whether or not they detect any purpose or justice in suffering. But some of us just see random suffering and injustice as part of the fabric of existence:

wild animals can't escape it, so why should we? Perhaps we fool ourselves with linear narratives about merit and reward distributed fairly across the lifespan and general population when we should know better about genetic "unfairness", accidents and chaos.

As I write these words I have recently turned sixty-one. I never thought I'd be this old and although in my psychological self-image I am still about twenty, in the mirror or shop window I am clearly, I think, a bit of an old codger. I have little hair left and a general demeanour of having seen far better days. No matter how vigorously I brush my teeth with whitening toothpaste they remain a little yellow. My recent appointment with the optician showed a need for a stronger prescription. A photograph of me at twenty-two shows a slim, tanned, not bad-looking young man on holiday in Spain, but it doesn't show the inwardly angst-ridden person I was. It's taken me a long time to become a bit more at peace with myself and in some ways it is true that life is good. But somehow simultaneously, ironically life has new problems. I can't do as much as I used to without tiredness; my sexual desire seems as high as ever but my performance doesn't match it; my memory for certain things isn't so good; I would like to change certain behaviours but many of the habits of a lifetime don't shift easily. I don't know quite "how to be": for example what to wear, or what to aim for in life. I am slightly afraid of becoming an eccentric Don Quixote character.

How long have I got? When people say "You're only as old as you feel" and "Sixty is the new forty" I am torn between contempt for such clichés and a concealed hope that they are true. Occasionally I become quite hypochondriacal, noticing a bump or bruise or ugly veins and shuddering at my declining aesthetic state and less than optimal health. How long have I got? How long do I want? Deep inside, the cogs of biological roulette are turning regardless of what "I" want. Yet I feel vaguely guilty for growing old, as if I could and should have prevented it. I could die at any time. I have forty years left at the very outside, probably around twenty, and quite possibly less. I may or may not suffer from one or another of the diseases of old age and the ignominy of the wretched nursing home. After I die I'll be remembered for a few years and then forgotten, as if I had never existed, or at best recede into fuzzy, distorted, scattered memories. I know we all face this but it feels personal, as if it's only happening to me.

A long, healthy and happy life is the main goal for many, even if the goal is merely implicit. Death is to be postponed for as long as possible and when it comes it should be a peaceful, sanitized death in bed. Most people in liberal Western democracies now expect to live into their eighties or beyond, as if sheer quantitative survival must be a good thing. This was not how Epicurus understood matters. In his account it is unimportant how long one lives; narrative accumulation of wisdom, say, is secondary to the completeness that comes from engagement with one's goals at any one time. Whereas for MacIntyre (2007) and champions of virtue, bringing the unity of life to completeness over time is what counts. Philosophers disagree about the values of lives that fluctuate from a good early life to an unhappier old age or vice versa. Clearly, an earlier failure can present as an "edifying misfortune" (Velleman 1991) leading to redemption, but late-life failures probably do not present the same opportunities for learning and change.

Given sufficient economic well-being and medical support, perhaps many older people will increasingly experience a preponderance of the good. But the remaining flies in the ointment of old age are all too clear to see. Schopenhauer's lament for the common "infirm and often wretched old age" has not yet been shown to be nonsense. Until much more effective cures are found, the older we get, the more susceptible to bodily and cognitive failures we become. In the sensory domain, deterioration in sight and hearing are the most common; in the cognitive, progressive memory failure.

Aristotle acknowledged that children must be exempt from any expectation of nobility. He did not accord the same privilege to those in old age. Indeed, in the *Rhetoric* he is distinctly negative about the character of the old, pessimistically regarding it as unlikely that much thriving takes place beyond one's prime. Happiness would be greater overall, he averred, if one did not outlive one's prime. The young still have potential; the old do not. Old age isn't necessarily bound to failure but it is commonly bound to fragility. If viability is characterized by health and robustness, then we may well suggest that the typical process of increasing fragility in later life is necessarily linked with increasing fallibility. (Indeed, quite literally, many older people fear falling since their bones are more brittle.) Summarizing the thinking of philosophers and writers on old age, Helen Small posits an inescapable double-think at work:

> Many of us spend more and more time, as we grow older, thinking about the fact that we are growing older and what it implies, but we also spend a great deal of time trying, more or less strenuously, *not* to think about that fact and what it implies. (2007: 272)

This dissonance between what we know and what we try not to know may be understood as a tragic failure to face reality, or simply as part of our natural fragility, or perhaps even as something like a design failure: consciousness gives us some prescience but this is outweighed by fear and avoidance.

Assumptions about the often unquestioned desirability of growing old are not without their critics. Take just one, the Japanese writer Yukio Mishima. Like some other young, warrior-oriented men, in contemporary and ancient societies, Mishima saw nothing good about getting old and dying a mundane death in bed; he regarded the old as ugly and far from wise, and ageing as inevitable decline. Death was not an inconvenient and unpalatable end point of the fading process of old age but the most important event, something to be regarded in heroic terms. For

Mishima these considerations led to his fatal decision and execu-
tion of ritual suicide (*seppuku*). Immediately after a failed *coup
d'état*, at the age of forty-five, he ritually disembowelled himself
and, by prior arrangement, had his head cut off, the decapitation
itself being botched at its first attempt. While not by any means the
same as the deaths of Empedocles, Socrates and Jesus, Mishima's
was based on a philosophy of life and death founded not on depression but on vigorous self-control and martial arts training. I am not
here advocating suicide to avoid growing old but illustrating the
point that passive ageing is not necessarily an inevitable or good
thing, and to think so is surely a failure of imagination. The current
growing trend for some older people who are suffering from incur-
able disease and terrible pain to terminate their lives is related to
Mishima's case by the moral principle of personal sovereignty over
one's life and death.

We might, with Maurice Merleau-Ponty, see our lives in time as
"the perpetual reiteration of the sequence of past, present and future
... as it were, a constant disappointment and failure" (1962: 453). It
is now a cliché to refer to past and future as illusions, or as mental
states only: the past full of regret and nostalgia, the future full of
hope and worry. The gloomiest among us may dwell on past and
future failures or imagined failures. But the present, "the now", even
the "eternal now" has become a fashionable and much sought-after
experience, particularly since the importation of Zen Buddhism
to the West in the 1960s but also increasingly in the practices of
meditation and mindfulness. Like many amateur meditators, I
have occasionally relaxed into a state of presence that felt distinctly
different from the typical everyday preoccupied mental state but
I know I have altogether failed to maintain a sense of heightened
presence in my everyday life. I cannot know if the Buddha actually
attained a state of freedom from the illusions of time but I can't
escape knowing that applied Buddhist philosophy hasn't worked
for me. I turn to Craig Bourne's (2006) philosophical analysis of

"presentism" for enlightenment but quickly become depressed on realizing that I simply cannot follow the text (yet another failure on my part), give up, and resign myself to living in the usual fuzzy mixture of past, present and future. I had vaguely looked forward to finally reading all those heavyweight books in my retirement but most of them will probably defeat me. If only I had saved money I could instead be travelling the world.

For some, the prospect of death itself is a disappointment. Given that each of us seems so unique and most accumulate large stores of memory, experience, knowledge and skill, it makes no intuitive or rational sense that all this is eventually wiped out. Quite naturally, many also fear death; indeed, all human cultures appear to have feared it and created rituals and explanations for addressing it. Some ancient traditions have recommended stoical acceptance or even welcomed death. Existentialists stress the defining importance of death as final. For Heidegger, "authentic, existentially projected being-toward-death" means "to be itself in the passionate anxious freedom towards death, which is free of all illusions of the they, factical, and certain of itself" ([1926] 2010: 255).

Statistics of average age at death and for increasing longevity can imply that a normal good life will now end at about eighty or ninety. There is now a sense that it is a success in itself to live to a ripe old age. Conversely, there is perhaps a superstition, suspicion or sadness about those who die in their sixties, fifties or younger, as if sheer dogged longevity trumps shorter lives. We may say "the good die young" but I doubt we really believe this. I suspect that often beneath the ritual outward sadness at shorter lives lurk ancient prejudices about biological inferiority, divine punishment or dark psychosomatic forces for which we are cryptically held responsible: a kind of counter-Mishima view.

Most religions contain theologies of death survival, and some frankly spurious spiritualism practices hold out hope of a life after death. For many in the Abrahamic traditions there is the prospect of a rewarding heaven or perfect paradise beyond flaws or suffering. For Hindus and some Buddhists there is the prospect of upward reincarnation. There being no evidence for such claims, one can choose to embrace them, dismiss them entirely or consign them to the category of harmless comfort-giving, or one can remain agnostic.

Refusing to accept the unacceptable flaw of mortality, some sign up and pay up for cryonic freezing and hope for potent future technologies to resurrect them. Increasingly, we witness a group of biogerontologists locked in a "war on ageing", who do not accept the inevitability of ageing, and death by about a hundred. Rather, they are serious about researching the causes of senescence and finding due therapies, and predict large advances within decades so that the lifespan may extend to hundreds of years and the quality of life and health for most of that time will be excellent. Here we may choose to admire the indomitable human spirit that stubbornly refuses to accept the inevitability of ultimate failure. Conversely we might interpret this attitude as a failure to face the ultimate reality, however frightening and disappointing, and furthermore as an act of unethical folly; if by any chance such research ever leads to a vastly increased lifespan, imagine the knock-on effects on world population, on intergenerational dynamics and other social and economic phenomena.

One might presume that after whatever ignominy and failure we face in this life, we can fairly "rest in peace" when we die. Hell (the latter-day destiny for all doomed souls) aside, it seems that a few of us who were deemed successful in life may succumb to post-humous failure in death. I refer to those celebrated persons who are exposed to revisionist biographies or slurs demonstrating by means of new evidence that the acclaimed deceased beat his wife, indulged in sexual perversions or was a racist, fascist, bigamist or plagiarist. It does not matter to the deceased but could be hurtful to family and fans. Think about the process of decanonization of saints: to become posthumously a failed saint. It is interesting that our posthumous reputation can matter so much to us, many driven and famous men especially being keen to promote their "legacy" as if anything less than immortality and standing out from the run of average human beings might constitute a failed life.

3. Collective human folly, sin and error

Collectively, we humans have long tried to understand ourselves and to envisage and create better societies. We have recognized deep fault lines in our collective behaviour, frequently leading to tragic outcomes, and analysed these tirelessly. Arguably, in spite of much social science, we are no closer to truly satisfactory analyses or solutions than we ever were, since chronic social and international problems dog us perpetually. We might usefully go back to the question of where all this began.

"Without the notion of a failed universe, the spectacle of injustice in every system would put even an abulic into a straitjacket" (Cioran 1998: 125). In other words, way beyond us, aeons before our personal, agentic responsibility developed, the foundations of the universe were laid. Not a perfect universe designed by a perfect God, it is a random universe creating within itself the forms that must follow from the ingredients and actions given. "Cosmogonic discomfort" is a term suggested by Cioran for these foundations. The universe is a mass of expanding and entropic forces and we human beings exist within this with all our apparently elevated consciousness and complex civilizations. We think we are a successful end point of millions of years of evolution, we glory in our cleverness, yet simultaneously lament our inability to remedy the tragedies independent of us and those of our making. Of course, it is true that we *are* in a sense the universe itself, composed of the same materials and reflecting back on itself. Human consciousness, containing not only self-preserving instincts but also what we might call "higher" emotions and reason, perceives and feels many dysfunctional and unjust phenomena to exist for which no clear and enduring corrective is available.

Somehow we reflect the expanding and entropic forces of our universe: we cannot help but develop and go forwards, yet we make a mess too. We *feel* that we are responsible and capable of necessary actions but often our actions are counterproductive. We claim to want justice but we perpetuate absurd injustices. Something beneath the level of our intellectual analysis, intentionality and will undermines us. "What I do is not the good I want to do" (Romans 7:19): this Pauline observation of our human obduracy is utterly central to the human predicament at both individual and collective levels and is essentially the same problem of *akrasia*.

Often our questions about life are unhelpfully grouped together and confused. Questions about the meaning of life proliferate: is it pointless and absurd, as Camus suggested? Theoretical battles over human nature torment us: are we essentially good, bad, neither or both? Deliberations over the best way to understand and meet social challenges continue unabated: what shall we do about crime, health, population, climate change? Many revel in the optimistic view that our progress is significant and continuing. But perhaps at best we imperfectly understand ourselves and "do our best" pragmatically to solve or reduce social problems.

I want to imagine here that we can succinctly and in a somewhat orderly fashion set out from the most general to the most personal some of the ways in which entropy, fallibility and failure plague and fool us from cosmic through evolutionary, religious, historical, civilizational, political, social, environmental, psychological and personal strata.

There is nothing we can do to reverse millions of years of our evolution. We have been *Homo sapiens* for a relatively brief time compared with the time span in which our origins lie. We share with animals the need to search for food and to reproduce, which entails predation upon others and avoidance of being predated upon. Aggression lies within our deep history, as does territoriality, competition and the tendency to relate positively to small groups of kin and to be somewhat suspicious of outsiders. Our physical evolution has bequeathed us many anatomical features and behaviours that do not always serve us well but that we cannot put aside, even if we can slowly modify some. Evolution occurs by using what is readily available and by gradual adaptation; it does not have the luxury of conscious design and redesign. Many features are carried forwards even when cumbersome or dysfunctional.

There are many dead or dying religions and the myths, sects and cults that go with them, as well as ongoing theological arguments for and against God. Secular atheism has grown but so too has fundamentalist and liberal religion. Lines of development can be traced from pantheism, polytheism and monotheism and the geography of religious belief and mission is fairly clear. I have no space here to attempt any detail. My own concise view is that humans once needed religion to explain what was frightening and unknown, and perhaps necessary for leadership and morality. But religious explanations and practices – a creator God, a son of God, walking on water, returning from death, orthodox and biblically preserved theologies, papal infallibility, to name a few – have become less and less credible with the growth of knowledge and science. While religion continues and even sometimes expands, it also becomes problematic and dangerous, and in some cases a taboo subject.

The strong case I want to put here, in the context of entropy, our species flaw and failure, is as follows. We can think of religion – belief in a supernatural God and his commands – as a kind of mimetic kluge. Religious ideas have been necessary, let's say; they were once the best we could come up with; they replicate themselves and are still doing so. Millions, if not billions, appear unable to live without them. I regard them as false but as filling an emotional need. In some cases they may be harmless and are quite understandable as providing comfort. But the most primitive, pre-scientific tenets of religion are not only redundant but an obstacle to self-understanding, international cooperation and understanding. I am not proposing the substitution of science for religion but the acceptance that human realities have changed dramatically in the past thousand and a half or three thousand years since the major Abrahamic religions appeared.

Unfortunately little if any rapprochement or progress is possible between hardened religious believers and atheists. I dislike the epithet "atheist" and would honestly prefer "one who believes she or he has outgrown superstitious explanations for the cosmos, life and human behaviour". (There's no getting around the cake-and-eat-it conundrum here: I may wish I could present an inoffen-sive, liberal, nice-guy persona but authenticity compels me to be honest.) Religion now utterly fails to offer a credible explanation. In the unending and often unedifying textual war between theists and so-called atheists, Victor Stenger has produced a refutation of God as good as any, by means of hypothesis-testing, which amounts to a verdict of the complete failure of theism:

> The large number of species results from the many, largely random attempts that evolution makes to produce a solution to the survival problem; many failures are to be expected as the bulk of these solutions fail. Many successes are marginal, leaving the species open to eventual extinction. We also know that mass extinctions have occurred several times as the result of natural catastrophes, such as meteorite strikes or geologic disruptions. (2008: 70)

This refutation of the argument for God's beneficent design will still not convince theists, of course. Nor will future meteor strikes or other global disasters (or cancer or AIDS) care who among us are theists or atheists. But the strong probability is that religious belief will gradually perish along with every other attempted but flawed solution.

As I have said, I think there is something resonant in the concept of original sin (or chronic human dysfunction, or species flaw); I am also sympathetic to belief in the reality of Buddha-like, individual, authentically embodied "mystical experience" or enlightenment (although caution is needed about this too). But religion itself, like all phenomena, decays over time. Religion may fade away completely within a few hundred years but in the meantime it remains a bug or virus, partially benign but ultimately a phenomenon of diminishing returns and a deadly fault in human affairs.

Impatient atheist readers may have skipped the above, but to what extent do we consider ourselves ahistorical? History might be considered in flux itself as a subject, with historians arguing about its proper contents and where it begins. The traditional conception of history as an objective record of significant events (usually of national and international significance but rarely, if ever, objective) has given way to an acknowledgement that most history has been written from the perspective of successful patriarchal societies. "Big history" now commences with the origins of the universe and tries to incorporate trends and phenomena that permeate all eras. Slightly less ambitiously, some accounts trace human expansion and development from hunter-gatherer times to the present, with an emphasis on tracking population growth and movement and civilizations' growth and decline. There is argument, too, about whether any lessons can be inferred from history that might serve as the basis for predictions. Some philosophers of history claim to detect patterns.

The German philosopher of history Oswald Spengler analysed world history in his magisterial *The Decline of the West* ([1922] 2006). Echoing Nietszche's "autumnal accent", he regarded "Entropy theory as the beginning of the destruction of that masterpiece of Western intelligence" (*ibid.*: 217), explaining that:

Every thing-become is mortal. Every thought, faith and science dies as soon as the spirits in whose words their "eternal truths" were true and necessary are extinguished. Dead, even, are the star-worlds which "appeared" to the astronomers of the Nile and the Euphrates, for our eye is different from theirs; and our eye in its turn is mortal.   (*Ibid.*: 90)

Much influenced by Spengler was the English historian Arnold Toynbee, whose multi-volume *A Study of History* was published in the 1930s and 1940s. Toynbee traced the negative paths of world history and foresaw doom and decay. Unfortunately for him he got into the business of making forecasts that quite clearly failed to materialize. Nonetheless, from before and after Gibbon's *The Decline and Fall of the Roman Empire*, we have histories in abundance of the rise and fall of civilizations. In spite of the assured tone of counter-doomsters such as Dan Gardner, who, in *Future Babble* (2011), dismisses Toynbee and many other prophets, we can see that empires do come into being and disappear. Twentieth-century history, with its two bloody world wars and many atrocities besides, surely *does* cast a large negative shadow over us, even if we conceded that overall violence is slowly declining.

Currently a large literature is available on the topic of the collapse of civilizations, Jared Diamond's *Collapse: How Societies Choose to Fail or Survive* (2005) being one of the most successful. The general tenor of these accounts is that human beings overreach themselves, fail to respect the environment, and gradually bring collapse on themselves through their own hubris. Combined with contemporary fears about climate change, resource depletion, population growth and international conflict, these analyses of past trends and current scenarios very commonly become grim prophecies about humanity's future prospects. Some, like those of the Gaia scientist James Lovelock, give us mere decades until disaster is caused by irreversible climate change, for example. This is not the place to attempt to address these debates but it must form part of our picture of human folly, of our collective moral failure and unwillingness to confront the likely consequences of present damaging actions.

Societal collapses could, of course, be a matter of chaos and inevitability. Plato wrote in his time about the collapse of Atlantis thousands of years ago from our own time, wanting to attribute moral (or immoral) reasons for its demise. Having carefully considered different kinds of "imperfect societies" in the *Republic*, Plato could not have known what archaeologists now suspect: that the island of Thera and its Minoan civilization (actually quite affluent and less patriarchal and aggressive than Greek society) was probably decimated by massive volcanic action and tsunamis. Modern scholars also propose alternative theories for other collapsed civilizations, or suggest that few civilizations actually completely perish; rather, they are transformed.

Anyone of my geography and generation (I was born in London in 1950) will have been familiar with globes and maps showing the large pink areas of the British Commonwealth. Although this had already begun crumbling, as a child I assumed that my country ruled, or had recently ruled, the world. Now, older Britons are still slow to come to terms with the reality of Britain as a small island with diminishing power. Year on year we are even dismayed to discover that our footballers and tennis players fail to win international trophies. Britain no longer heads an empire consisting of many colonies; instead, it is a multicultural nation of gradually declining wealth and influence. It may not exactly be a "failed nation", or even a poor one, but it seems well past its best. "Broken Britain" may be more of a political slogan than real but the notion of a failing society has some credence. This is probably true of most other European nations, many of which once had extensive empires. My point is, of course, that change, flux or entropy does appear to rule in these matters. The territorial or ideological expansionism of so many nations isn't sustainable in the long run, and many now forecast the demise of the USA as China, India and South American economies and societies begin to flourish. Meanwhile, Britain may remain a locus of the fantasized good life for many immigrants at the same time as many Britons fantasize about a more successful life elsewhere.

There is obviously no perfect country, no country free from failure or failures. Indeed, all probably have their characteristic "failure style". The British are sometimes said to hate or fear success, or consider it vulgar. Americans, on the other hand, appear to make it central and to pursue and celebrate it (while internally playing down their own inevitable poverty problems). Germany tends towards economic success even while it is still only too aware of its collective moral failure many decades ago. Italy is celebrated for its aesthetic flair and sexiness while all too aware of a continuing underbelly of Mafia-style corruption. Japan is interesting for its combined striving for economic success and heightened sense of shame at collective and individual failure, the latter often resulting in concealment of lost jobs and suicide. Anyone interested in an academic comparison of Japanese and American reactions to failure can consult a paper structured according to strict experimental design (Heine *et al.* 2001).

As Noam Chomsky demonstrates, "failed states" were so designated by the USA and allies to refer to countries perceived as a threat to their security. The definition of such failure includes the "inability or unwillingness to protect their own citizens from violence"; "their tendency to regard themselves as being beyond the reach of domestic or international law"; and "democratic deficit" (2007: 2). The USA has often so characterized Haiti and Iraq, with past foreign policy also invoking a terminology of rogue states and axis of evil variously to condemn North Korea, Iran and Iraq. Chomsky argues that both internal American political realities and aggressive American foreign policy suggest that the USA itself could be considered a failed state. In other words, this kind of failure is usually defined by those in power. But few even now refer to the USA as an evil state for its treatment ("extermination" as many would frankly call it) of its Native American inhabitants. Chomsky argues that the USA may be the paramount case of a nation representing a threat to world order.

If you want to ask if national and international politics really matter to the individual in terms of success and failure, it quite clearly does. Born at the "wrong time" and in the "wrong place", your life chances will almost certainly be very poor compared with millions of others lucky enough to have been born into relatively affluent democracies. It matters too, of course, into which part of your society you are born. Promoters of free-market capitalism, of the American can-do attitude, want us all to believe we can pull ourselves up by our bootstraps: anyone can do well, make their own fortune. It is true to say that a minuscule percentage can and does rise from dire poverty but the mathematics of significant economic success dictate that very few can get to or stay at the top.

In their much-lauded *The Spirit Level* (2009), Richard Wilkinson and Kate Pickett collated data from many countries, which they put forward as the foundation for an "evidence-based politics". Their thesis is that more equal societies perform better and are experienced as more convivial on a variety of measures than unequal societies, the Scandinavian countries usually coming out best of all. Putting it quite simply, material success almost always accompanies what they call "social failure". In stark terms:

> We can fail to prevent catastrophic global warming, we can allow our societies to become increasingly anti-social and fail to understand the processes involved. We can fail to stand up to the tiny minority of the rich whose misplaced idea of self-interest makes them feel threatened by a more democratic and egalitarian world. *(Ibid.*: 264)

63

The rich and other critics of their data and their interpretation are squeamish about restraining free-market capitalism and wealth distribution. What is lacking is political will, or collective conative failure, in which we are all implicated.

We like to think of *Homo sapiens* as a pretty clever and resourceful species and, of course, as wise. We marvel at the achievements of humanity, at our rationality, altruism and our potential for overcoming all obstacles. But these achievements are spotty and subject to wear and tear. The category of "civilization" is one of our largest achievements. However, the radical anarchist John Zerzan (sometimes dubbed an anarcho-primitivist philosopher), regarding civilization as pathological, speaks of "the failure of symbolic thought", of our "fall into representation" and "fundamental falsification" (2002: 2). "More of what has failed us for so long can hardly be the answer" (*ibid.*: 16). For Zerzan, the remedy, to be brought about by worldwide anti-capitalist revolution, is an extreme anarchistic return to natural conditions, including sensually rich, prelinguistic consciousness. For many (not only capitalists but all who live and profit by more-of-the-same intellectual wrangling), such a scenario is anathema. Some nature mystics, radical environmentalists, eco-feminists and end-time survivalists share similar views, if with very different nuances. But even if we agree that the trance that language holds us in is a large part of our species' or social problem, it seems reasonable to argue that the *uber-kluge* of civilization is not reversible, nor is symbolic thought at all likely to obligingly wither. Additionally, very few of us would cope with the kinds of massive changes proposed. I, for one, an ageing, thoroughly impractical urbanite dependent on spectacles and blood pressure and other tablets, wouldn't last five minutes. This doesn't automatically invalidate Zerzan's argument but suggests that his remedy would have extremely high human costs.

Looking very briefly at some mainstream Western political philosophers across the centuries, we see a mixture of foci, aspirations and blind spots. The Platonic recipe of philosophers as rulers has some appeal (especially against today's typically pragmatic, anti-intellectual political leaders) but Plato's condoning of the "noble lie" in politics must be regarded as an extremely slippery slope; and his indifference to the plight of slaves and women shows his geo-temporal limits. Niccolò Machiavelli, still admired in some quarters for his amoral pragmatism, left us complacent about the so-called need for "dirty hands" in politics. Recognizing nature as a "state of war", Hobbes argued that only absolute sovereignty of rule could contain and protect citizens for whom life was otherwise "solitary, poore, nasty, brutish and short". Arguments have raged unresolved for centuries over questions of equality, human rights, property, virtue, universal morality, the meaning of history, alienation, justice and emancipation.

Perhaps not until Mary Wollstonecraft was the equality of men and women taken seriously, along with real consideration of the plight of the poor. Marx stands out for his attempt to create a radical analysis of history, class struggle and contemporary working conditions, and his revolutionary recommendations. But communism is now widely dismissed as a failed philosophy and socioeconomic experiment, indeed by many Americans as pure evil. Yet simultaneously we have had instances of dire economic and moral failure of runaway free-market capitalism with no lessons learnt from it, as if we must accept the tacit assumption of capitalism that human beings must be free to compete, whatever the outcomes. This is exactly the theme of Andrew Ross Sorkin's *Too Big to Fail* (2010), charting the events of 2008–9: the hubris of American bankers, the collapse of Lehman Brothers' banking empire and dire economic effects for much of the world.

Scott Sandage, in *Born Losers* (2005), his history of failure in America, is quite frank about American capitalism and the distribution of blame for success and failure:

The self-made man who fulfilled his contracts embodied the free agent – individualism made flesh – but so did the broken man who could not fulfil them. Twins were born in ante-bellum America; success and failure grew up as the Romulus and Remus of capitalism. Failure was intrinsic, not antithetical, to the culture of individualism. "Not sinking" took both self-reliance and self-criticism, lest a dream become a nightmare.   (*Ibid*.: 67)

That natural inequality is vastly better than forced equality is now the widely accepted view in most countries, in spite of the ongoing democratic farce of typical pseudo-choices between left- or right-leaning political parties. We also create dead-end notions of "third way" politics. My inference from the long history of political philosophy and our current plight is that we fail to overcome the deep-seated pluralism in human nature (with some philosophers such as Berlin and Gray arguing the wisdom of pluralism being accepted); and that the serious flaws of brute tribalism, competition, inequality and war seem unlikely to reduce significantly in a hurry.

The political philosopher John Dunn asks why we have politics at all. Drawing on theories of "original sin or moral error" (which he also refers to as "radical fatalism"), he asks if "there is a way in which human beings should behave but in which most of them conspicuously fail to" (2000: 19). This is in contrast to

the view that all human beings, now and for the rest of their earthly existence, will continue to be driven to act in a manner deeply malign towards one another, and that what will compel them to do so is the cruelty, greed, pride and treachery at the very core of their personalities.   (*Ibid*.: 347)

For Dunn, modern democracy for all its shortcomings is at least the beginning of a possible solution. I do not subscribe to quite such radical fatalism but I suspect that entrenched human moral failure and folly will indeed persist indefinitely.

For the vast majority of us, our environment is our house (if we have one), neighbourhood and country. Our experience of the environment is the "concrete jungle" for urban dwellers, and villages and farmlands for a dwindling minority. We are affected by our local climate and daily weather and in certain areas many millions are deeply affected by droughts or other extreme weather events. Many live choicelessly close to volcanoes, earthquake zones and areas subject to flooding; some have little choice but to live uncomfortably close to airports, noisy major roads and nuclear power plants. Those of us lucky enough to take holidays to exotic, paradise-like locations, usually spread more than our share of carbon emissions in the process. A tiny and disproportionately rich minority own many houses and live and move where they choose. Despite significant migration, the vast majority live close to where they were born.

The "environment" means different things to each of us. Those unlucky enough to live in endangered areas already experience the real threat of climate change as they lose their livelihood owing to flooding, droughts and inhospitable temperature increases. Perhaps most of us feel a mixture of worry, responsibility, guilt, helplessness, hope and some scepticism about climate change. The information about it comes from distant scientists or popular media sources; politicians appear to fail to respond to it with due urgency; capitalism has always relied on economic growth that increases carbon emissions; world population increases and most people dislike being told how many children they can have, but population is a causative factor in climate change. By definition, anthropogenic climate change is "our fault" and our failure to address its possibly devastating consequences in a timely manner may lead to a gravely compromised future habitat. Yet this is a conundrum if we follow the evolutionary logic that human beings are simply doing what all life forms do: adapting, playing to our advantages, surviving, flourishing. Some religions have told us that we are masters of creation and should multiply. We appear to be at a historical point where we must pull together internationally and embrace austerity, when intergroup conflict and affluence pursuit are our norms. Even Gardner (2011), as a debunker of most prophecies, agrees that we can't afford to judge this climate-change scenario incorrectly.

The moral philosopher Stephen Gardiner (2011) employs the metaphor of a "perfect moral storm" for the three sites of moral corruption that coincide in this gathering storm of climate-change catastrophe: the buck-passing of costs to the developing world by the affluent nations; buck-passing the problem to future genera-tions; and our failure to grasp and combine key scientific knowl-edge and issues of international justice. Gardiner is quite clear in his highly detailed ethical analysis that our glaring failure to address the climate-change problem is a radical moral failure at both political and personal levels.

At the everyday sub-political level, work of one kind or another is almost universal. For the majority, work means the "9 to 5" or variations on that. It is hailed by capitalists as an engine of economic growth and by moralists and others as the thing that gives us purpose, makes us human, yet for many work really is wage slavery. Picture those millennia of evolution leading to complex human consciousness, and all that parental care and education for each individual, and what does it amount to? How many millions of us spend every day commuting, then spending eight hours or so in sedentary prostration before the computer, scanning the screen, clicking the mouse, attending to emails, bureaucratic demands, invoices and so on? Of course, work isn't like this for all, and some say they enjoy it. For a few very privileged businesspeople, enter-tainers and sportspeople, work is altogether a different matter. Compare the egregiously overpaid footballer, for example, occa-sionally successful in kicking a piece of leather between two posts, or assisting in this operation, with the world's hard-labouring masses living in poverty. If that isn't an absurd moral failure, what is? Not only religion but football too is the opium of the people.

For millions, work is what most of their time is dedicated to, and often for up to fifty years or more. How did humanity come to this state of mind-bogglingly boring, imprisoning and degrading activity? Bound together by work, mortgages, television and so-called leisure, most of us, in spite of Sartrean principles of freedom, appear to have little choice but to become institutionalized, doing what we do not wish to do, while paradoxically longing to escape.

Plato and Aristotle had a lot to say, often in derogatory and ambivalent terms, about work and different kinds or levels of workers. Christianity bequeathed us the idea of work as curse and duty, even converting it via the writings of Luther and Calvin into the Protestant work ethic, the selfless dedication of effort to God. Marx contextualized and critiqued work differently yet again, recommending its reconceptualization into community needs, creative individual fulfilment and leisure. It may appear romantic and impractical to many to call for an overhaul of the dehumanizing nature of modern institutions' work cultures. On observing how so often the joyful and curious young person is dulled by compulsory education and desk-bound routines from their late teens or twenties into their sixties (the "toil-filled years"), I think it is necessary, however, that we at least ask whether work fails us in our needs and aspirations. Are the twenty-first century's work routines really the best we can come up with? The capitalist juggernaut and sheer unimaginative tradition crushes the human spirit in millions of cases. The mismatch between the development, feelings and needs of the soft machine and the daily demands of a capitalism indifferent to these ("bioderegulation", some call it) is arguably a flaw in our lifestyle so immense that we barely pause seriously to consider alternatives.

Camus's *The Myth of Sisyphus* ([1942] 1975) dwells on the absurdities of human existence, many of them found in the daily routines of pointless work. We are, says Camus, carried along by time, occasionally realizing that we are merely growing older. The world is made up of illusions, irrationality, futile repetitions and absurdities that force us to ask why we don't commit suicide. Writing of the existentialist philosopher Karl Jaspers, Camus argues:

> He knows that we can achieve nothing that will transcend the fatal game of appearances. He knows that the end of the mind is failure. He tarries over the spiritual adventures revealed by history and pitilessly discloses the flaw in each system … in this ravaged world. (*Ibid.*: 29)

In the domain of close relationships we might cynically speak of ourselves as flawed people seeking perfect understanding and acceptance from others. Few of us can live entirely alone and yet the jocular "can't live with them, can't live without them" observation reveals just how fragile desired relationships can be. Here we probably have a curve of very successful through tolerable to terrible relational experiences, many coming to painful ends. We can analyse this and offer couple counselling for it with some success but it seems that a substantial element of relationship failure will always be with us. Entropy seems to account for the state of being in love converting into a range of states of intermittent happiness, compromise and conflict. Basic faults and flaws in either partner often spell long-term failure, as if unconsciously some had advertised "Irredeemably fucked-up sinner/failure seeks similar". Indeed, despite all the hard work put in by many relationship partners, it is as if unconsciously one or both of them were always going to sabotage it. Yet the institution persists and alternative arrangements and experiments appear to have had no greater success rate. Many early Greek philosophers warned against the madness and frenzy of sex and its consequences, celibacy is a key characteristic for many Christian and Buddhist priests, and Schopenhauer, while recognizing "the madness of carnal desire", regularly frequented a brothel rather than marrying.

We fail to understand whether it is life itself or the kinds of societies we construct that fosters so much cruelty and suffering. But we do know that personal psychological suffering is widespread. For well over a hundred years now we have had various talking therapies and well before those we have had psychiatric endeavours. We still flounder in trying to pin down the real causes of depression and anxiety, and hundreds of other forms of psychological pain. The clinical psychologist Richard Bentall says of medical psychiatry:

> More than a century of endeavour has not led to improvements in outcomes for patients with severe mental illness. People experiencing psychotic symptoms in countries with few mental health professionals do better than patients in countries with well-resourced psychiatric services.
>
> (2010: 24)

Interestingly, Bentall uses theological language to further indict psychiatry when he says "psychiatry's greatest sin has been to crush hope in those it has claimed to care for" (*ibid.*: 288).

Passionate and damning though they are, such words conceal much. The "virtue of kindness" that Bentall sees in some forms of psychotherapy and in service users' involvement in their own support does not reveal the sheer, stubborn suffering that is often helped by nothing and by no one, or is only partly ameliorated in a hit-or-miss way. Concealed is our ignorance about or failure to concur on the complex causes of mental distress. Concealed here are the ongoing turf wars over status and salaries between psychiatrists and clinical psychologists and between the hundreds of different talking therapies and their advocates. (I have, for example, seen some people helped by free drugs when expensive talking therapy did not work.) Concealed or denied is the probability, shall we say, that psychiatrists, psychologists, psychotherapists and counsellors, however well meaning, psychoanalysed and professionalized themselves, are at root as fucked-up as anyone else: how could it be otherwise in this vale of tears? Of course this dim view can be and is refuted as cynicism (with a small "c") by those who profit from keeping false hope alive. But arguably it is only by allowing in the darkest data of the human condition that we have any chance of real progress; and, after all, there may well be no "final solution" to psychological suffering.

How do all the above considerations affect the individual? Perhaps most of us get along without much sustained thought about cosmological, evolutionary, historical, political, economic and other matters. It is certainly argued by many philosophers and psychologists that the typical human being has poor reasoning and makes many cognitive errors. We might also suggest that our universe, although knowable, can be fully understood only via the details of specialized disciplines that most of us cannot or do not have time to master. One can garner only the barest, flimsiest gist of cosmology, evolution, religion and so on. Knowledge grows and accumulates rapidly and one cannot keep up with it. It is hardly surprising if the average human mind fails to grasp accurately the sweep of history, religion and similar phenomena. Even experts disagree, of course. Yet we tend to say that all this doesn't matter, that everyone's opinion is equally valuable, for example on issues of religion and politics. We hate the idea – or at least we disown it – that the knowledge and judgement of some people may be inferior to that of others.

Regardless of whether we do spend much time in such thoughts, arguably we are always deeply affected by what they refer to. Indeed, for Sartre and many other philosophers it may become unthinkable that one would shut out claims on one's social consciousness. You may decide to become a Jehovah's Witness or Scientologist on the basis of a chance meeting with an enthusiast, and your life course takes a commensurate turn (when a comprehensive analysis of world religions would have better enlightened you). You may decide that this is a failed universe and an absurd existence and become depressed or kill yourself (when certain philosophical texts can offer both disputatious and consoling perspectives on such matters). You may assume as many do that you are a failure because you have promiscuous thoughts or hate work (when many texts might offer you explanations from evolutionary psychology or Marxism, or even occupational psychology, that suggest these are extremely common sentiments that can be accounted for).

Finding our lives a little too bewildering, stressful or unsatisfying, many of us turn to religion, counselling, hedonistic escapism, the lottery. It seems very likely that we do what Marcus (2008) says we do: like evolutionary adaptation, we take whatever is to hand in the context in which we live and we fallibly use it to help us get by, and often we become attached to such adopted beliefs and practices and fail to outgrow them even when they are no longer useful; indeed we often cling to beliefs and institutions all the more as we anxiously sense their fallibility. The bits and pieces of half-digested knowledge we pick up in our lives serve as kluges. They work in a fashion and may help us to feel that we are coping successfully.

My own chance bricolage of beliefs includes atheism, which is not merely a swipe at the religious but standing up for all that life, reading and reason tells me. It includes a strong sense of absurdity, negativity and humour, which is probably a personality trait compounded by early-life experiences but also drawn from many Sisyphean job situations. I am, politically, passively left-leaning in so far as I despise the greed, deceptiveness and other madnesses of consumerist capitalism, and this I learned from my father. Increasingly, I am an armchair anarchist. I have something like an old-hippie leaning towards a laidback lifestyle, moderate hedonism and mysticism (particularly Krishnamurti), which is all to do with when and where I was born and what I have accidentally read. I have some fondness for the world of counselling and psychotherapy, not for its crazier theories, romantic clichés and wild claims or for its self-importance but for the simple compassionate pragmatism of its best practitioners and the fact that little else is available for many who suffer.

My flaws have made it hard for me (whatever the true distinction between "my flaws" and "me" may be) to change my views and behaviour in later life. Having mostly lived in lower-middle-class England, I have no deep, authentic feeling for those who live in oppressed areas and conditions. I have struggled through an era of sometimes militant feminism and have often failed to appreciate women's angrier claims. But I am increasingly persuaded – mainly by observation and reading, partly (incidentally) by primal therapy – that millennia of patriarchy are responsible for much human immiseration; perhaps even that patriarchal emotion-suppression and empathic failure is one of the main roots of chronic human pathology and that a return to an emotion-freeing and emotion-respecting culture is necessary.

I infer from my own experiences, correctly or incorrectly, that much of what is wrong with human beings and human affairs is not corrected by education, reason or exhortation but by time, necessity and gradual insight. It has been said that although we sometimes admit to retrospective error, no one ever admits in mid-sentence, "Oh, I am wrong!" Unfortunately, this default tactic of blustering on as usual may not work in the case of climate change, where time is running out. I also realize, as we all must, that frequently we do not, apparently *cannot*, see eye to eye: individuals and groups have their own stubborn bricolage of experiences, beliefs and affiliations and many of these are in serious conflict with others'. Yet even if (and this will never happen) we agreed to a system of universal rational education that included a philosophical analysis of common cognitive errors, something deep within us would probably remain resistant to any radical change.

Personally, I am convinced that in spite of our countervailing virtues and partial progress we human beings have a serious, chronic, unaddressed failure at our core. We may baulk at calling it original sin or a species flaw but there is arguably something curiously rotten or warped deep down inside most of us: our readiness to lie, to dissimulate, to let our integrity crumble, to avoid speaking the truth. Augustine propounded the view that *all* lying is sinful, yet probably all humans lie. Wittgenstein recognized the rarity of honesty and was known to often be unusually truthful. Like most of us, my nerve fails me in many everyday situations that call for *parrhēsia* (freely speaking one's mind) for fear of causing offence or incurring serious social costs. The Cynic Diogenes referred to this outspokenness as "mankind's most beautiful thing" and Nietszche and Foucault also explicitly espoused it. Socrates, Jesus and many others have paid with their lives for speaking what they considered the truth regardless of consequences. Many contemporary protestors and whistle-blowers have lost their lives or jobs for speaking out.

Religious fundamentalists have added a recent layer of what is effectively censorship to a long-standing "anti-*parrhēsic*" tradition. Mostly *parrhēsia* is a rare commodity and lack of it points to deep-seated moral failure, cowardice, inauthenticity and bad faith. It may be difficult to distinguish between hate-motivated fascist groups who attempt to hijack the right to speak plainly and be heard on the one hand, and sincere and thoughtful spokespeople on the other. Much ethical agonizing goes into this problem. But the combined forces of the over-sensitive and the insensitive render much daily life highly inauthentic in schools, in the workplace, in politics and elsewhere. Most of us tacitly accept the necessity of lies and disingenuousness and yet it must also strike us as quite astonishing that we cannot get along without lies, that we choose to live (or believe we have no choice but to live) by suppressing honesty.

4. The tragic arts

Awareness of failures on all levels is illustrated abundantly in religion, philosophy, literature and art. In this chapter I look at failure through the lens of many of our artistic and creative media, mainly poetry, drama, novels, visual art, film and comedy. Obviously this is a highly selective look. Interestingly, Plato was somewhat hostile to the arts, regarding them as glamorizing the illusory and impeding the search for truth. We know, however, from the Bible and many other sources that the arts in all their forms were always the chief means of reflecting on human misfortunes and provoking popular engagement with tragic themes.

In her extremely scholarly *The Fragility of Goodness* (2001), the philosopher Martha Nussbaum takes as her theme the "moral luck" that challenges the "aspiration to rational self-sufficiency" of so many early Greek philosophers and indeed poets. Greek tragedy, often differing sharply from contemporary philosophy, showed that bad things often happen to good people. Regardless of how good we strive to be, events outside our control can seriously knock us back. Even the most disciplined Stoics and others aspiring by the exercise of reason to be immune to adversity may be tested beyond their powers of endurance and brought low: this has often offended the sensibilities of philosophers such as Aristotle and Kant. However we arrange circumstances we cannot foresee all potential tests of fate, shocks and misfortunes, and this is the stuff of a great deal of literature and art. Furthermore, just as the virtuous may fall, so the deviant and undeserving may prosper. For example, the lifelong dissolute character may enjoy a long healthy life while the person observing all solid health advice may be susceptible to disease or early death. Whatever philosophical principles are adopted, the arbitrariness of moral luck can cut through them. As Nussbaum says, the good life is always vulnerable to moral luck. And it is just this element of chance and unpredictability that has engaged audiences for many centuries.

Arguably more than most philosophers, the pessimistic Schopenhauer has directly influenced novelists and dramatists such as Beckett, Chekhov, Conrad, Hardy, Mann, Proust, Tolstoy and Zola, among others. A small number of philosophers have also been novelists (e.g. Simone de Beauvoir, Camus, Iris Murdoch and Sartre), consciously exploring philosophical themes in fiction. I have used the word "tragic" here but we might remember that literature takes many forms, even among those exploring features of existential failure. Nietszche distinguished between Appollonian and Dionysian arts, the former characterized by sculpture, the latter by music, corresponding somewhat to dreams and drunkenness. Benjamin distinguished between *Trauerspiel* (the play of mourning, or melancholy) and tragedy, regarding the writer of the former as "sorrowful investigator" and melancholy as proceeding necessarily from the Fall (Pensky 2001). My concern here is with our longstanding melancholy legacy as a flawed species *and* numerous examples of personal, situational and global failures.

Discussing tragedy, Adrian Poole calls attention to the place of the fatal error and fatal flaw connoted by Aristotle's *hamartia*:

> Others translate *hamartia* more simply as "fault", "mistake", or "error". And however much of a character's *propensity* to error we read into the concept, the primary emphasis seems to be on the error itself, the fault committed. To take a mild example, it's like a tennis serve that falls on the wrong side

of the line ("Fault!"). To take a graver example, Philoctetes wanders off the beaten path and into a sacred shrine guarded by a snake, who punishes his "error". (2005: 46)

As existentialist philosopher William Barrett has it, we collectively exist:

in a state of "fallen-ness" (*Verfallenheit*), according to Heidegger, in the sense that we are as yet below the level of existence to which it is possible for us to rise. ... But, as happened to Ivan Ilyich in Tolstoy's story, such things as death and anxiety intrude upon this fallen state, destroy our sheltered position of simply being one among many, and reveal to us our own existence as fearfully and irremediably our own". (1961: 196)

John Calder (2001), presenting the plays, novels and life of Samuel Beckett as philosophy, combines notions of philosophy as fiction and failure as art, as well as inferring an ethic of Stoicism from Beckett's work. In his view, Beckett regarded success and failure as "neither significant nor different, as they lead inevitably to the same end. Success is only a trap, offering a temporary and false security which can crumble away at any time". Further, "there is neither fault nor shame in failure. The cause, more often than not ... is accident ... part of the chaos and general mess of all existence" (*ibid.*: 9). Beckett himself had said that for the artist "failure is his world" (quoted in *ibid.*: 138). And of course Beckett has left us, from *Worstward Ho*, with what has unfortunately become the tediously over-quoted "Ever tried. Ever failed. No matter. Try again. Fail again. Fail better."

The American novelist Paul Auster (1998), in the first few pages of an autobiographical text, says that at one stage "everything I touched turned to failure. My marriage ended in divorce, my work as a writer foundered, and I was overwhelmed by money problems" (1998: 3); and "my relationship to money had always been flawed" (*ibid.*: 3). Of his warring and ultimately divorced parents, he says, "money was the fault line" (*ibid.*: 7). Then an aspiring writer enduring odd jobs, unlikely money-making schemes and poverty in a tragic admixture, Auster became an outstanding critical and commercial success on the international scene.

Back at the beginning, one of our very oldest works of literature is *The Epic of Gilgamesh*, thought to date from about 2000 BCE. In this poem from the Middle East the hero, Gilgamesh, is a powerful warrior who comes to love Enkidu, initially a rival. When Enkidu dies Gilgamesh is distraught and launches into a quest for immortality, which of course must fail. Also in the story are fragments about the guile of a woman, and a great flood. Homer's *Iliad* and *Odyssey*, thought to date from the eighth century BCE, contain the themes of fate, homecoming, wrath, glory and honour, and adventure, travel, intrigue, a voyage to the underworld, disguise and personal weakness, respectively. Both include gods and heroes. The Bible too contains many stories of migration, war, heroes, morality, prophets and gods, rewards and punishments. All these literary sources suggest preoccupations with questing, mortality, agonizing, battles and hopes, righteousness and wickedness. All are dominated by male characters. Dante's fourteenth century CE allegorical epic poem *The Divine Comedy* shows a Christian worldview of hell, purgatory and heaven characterized by themes of darkness, fear, deadly sins, self-indulgence, violence and malice, and love. Shakespeare's tragedy *Macbeth* distils the all too human elements of vanity, envy and guilt, played out around the murder of King Duncan and the inevitable escalation of killing, of Macbeth's own downfall and death. While we have clearly had great shifts across centuries of literature, an element of dissatisfaction, bewildered trauma, suffering and hope of redemption is rarely far away.

We are often told that humans are myth-making creatures. Clearly we are. We are told we *need* myths and stories. About this I'm less sure; or rather I want to know *why* so many of us apparently need them. After all, fiction is fiction, akin to deception, even though we find it entertaining or morale-boosting. Aristotle asserted that all of us reach for understanding by our very nature:

> It is because of wonder that human beings undertake philosophy, both now and at its origins ... The person who is at a loss and in a state of wonder thinks he fails to grasp something; this is why the lover of stories is in a sense a philosopher, for stories are composed out of wonders.　　　(Nussbaum 2001: 259)

Wonder is not the same thing as being at a loss or failing to grasp something. My conjecture is that this sense of loss and needing to understand has particular roots that we can link with the earliest literature and its themes. Perhaps prototypical literature and the arts arose around a time of significant migrations, loss of home, wars and deaths, when human consciousness became acutely aware of matters not being axiomatically happy. The creation of myths about heroes, gods and God seems to fit a pattern of seeking reassurance in narratives that could embody explanations when scientific knowledge was slight and anxieties were high. Stories may contain philosophies; even today fiction is vastly more popular than philosophy. But fiction is also more popular than science. Fiction, drama and poetry evidently meet a deep emotional need, just as religion does. But what is it about human beings, about human consciousness, that found and finds existence in itself some sort of failure or insufficiency? Presumably animals do not feel this way. Human beings in love, in action and in mystical union do not feel they are failing to grasp something. Is it only human beings with too much surplus time and thought, and too little absorption in necessity, who fail to grasp "something"?

In his poem "Burnt Norton", T. S. Eliot included the memorable lines "human kind ... cannot bear very much reality" and "dessication of the world of sense". Did our language-heavy consciousness sever us from direct experience; did it fail us? Did that which distinguished us from animals and launched our amazingly complex civilizations simultaneously become perhaps our gravest flaw?

How does each of us come to meaningful literature, when we do? In my own adolescent angst, finding life dry, difficult and rather pointless, it was reading certain texts at school and the accidental discovery of certain authors that brought me out of dire misery. I was indeed at a loss and failing to grasp something. Variously, Fyodor Dostoevsky, Eliot, Thomas Hardy, Ernest Hemingway, Aldous Huxley, D. H. Lawrence, George Orwell and Dylan Thomas all gave me a sense, however fuzzy, of others grappling seriously with life's failures. Very few real people of my acquaintance seemed to engage in such thoughts, religion seemed too fantastical and its scriptures too removed from the present, and most philosophy far too abstruse to be helpful. But some poetry and novels pointed the way or reflected the being at a loss and in a state of wonder. Only much, much later did any science and history start to answer some of my burning questions.

Both as an adolescent and now I find myself very busy-minded, flitting from one preoccupation to another. I puzzle over difficult aspects of life, I search for answers, I engage in various projects, and I have struggled to find peace and meaning in jobs and relationships. W. B. Yeats's "I have attempted many things/And not a thing is done" captures some of the sense of being at a loss, one's disappointed heart forever distracting from one's best efforts.

Eliot's *The Waste Land*, published in 1922, conveys much of the aridity of modern life:

A crowd flowed over London Bridge, so many,
I had not thought death had undone so many.

> I can connect
> Nothing with nothing.

We studied this at school for an A-level exam and it hit me in two ways. First, what Eliot seemed to be saying (behind many obscure references) was that modern life was some kind of failure: urban life, work, marriage and sex were all disappointing, and death hovered over everything. But second, how was it that such a poem, apparently so critical of our way of life, was being held up as an example of great literature by the mainstream school system? Were we expected to remain detached about it, and not be personally, emotionally affected? Should one praise the state education system for exposing young people to challenging literature, or suspect it of not actually getting it: that is, that some of us might be depressed by it or stimulated to serious protest?

I left school at eighteen and my first job in the "Unreal City" required me to walk over Blackfriars Bridge and sit in a tiny office doing utterly soul-destroying bureaucratic work. Since no one can control for subjective associations and reactions, I can report that lines from Dylan Thomas echoed in my head at that time; Gaugin's example of self-exile also featured there; the films *Lord of the Flies* (1963), *If* (1968) and *Zabriskie Point* (1970) all played a part in my mistrust of society and its grown-ups. The nuclear threat and Vietnam featured prominently around that time, as did the student riots in Paris in 1968. Countercultural politics, drugs, art and literature were all part of the ferment of a rejection of a society that appeared to be a manifest failure: materially rich but failing to nurture the human spirit.

Awareness of and protest against materialist values was evident well before the 1960s, however (indeed, recall the Cynics from well over 2,000 years ago). In 1949, Arthur Miller's play *Death of a Salesman* had its premiere. It remains a classic study of failure at several levels. Its main character, Willy Loman from Brooklyn, is at sixty-three fired from his sales job of thirty-six years. He has been struggling with work and debt, having accidents and, his wife finds, planning suicide. Like many others he can be perceived as being failed by the American consumerist dream that pushed so many into unrealistic aspirations that entailed high mortgages and debts and ended up simply exhausting them, breaking their morale. Willy is disappointed in his two sons, neither of whom is a success: one flunked maths at school, a failure that dogs him; the other is described by their mother as a "philandering bum". So this extremely sad play ends in Willy's death and haunting themes about a flawed, dehumanizing capitalism and its brutal competitiveness, a somewhat deluded, failed salesman and the transgenerational transmission of flaws (the "sins" of the fathers). Willy is truly finished, washed up, and we are faced with difficult questions about causes and casualties.

We might pause here to consider certain perennial philosophical themes. There is some conceptual entropy at work in getting from the proposed good life of early Greek philosophers to the consumerist dystopia of modernity. The concept of happiness is distorted over time, it becomes a mere right and ends in the superficial hedonism so ubiquitous today. The concept of authenticity, of being true to oneself, falters and fails across time, so that individuals end up chasing it as a chimera, as yet another elusive goal. The examined life deteriorates into the ridiculous ritual of long unproductive years on the analyst's couch, Woody Allen-style, and the mesmerising jargon that accompanies it.

We can compare two short classic novels for themes of failure: Tolstoy's *The Death of Ivan Ilyich* (originally published in 1886) and Camus' *The Fall* (published in 1956). What these have in common is a male lead character who is an outward success, in both cases quite prominent in the legal profession. In the first, Ivan Ilyich works very hard to elevate himself in society and career, and to marry suitably. He is convinced he has made all the right moves and yet he is haunted by a sense of failure, is not much loved, and, following an injury, he falls ill and dies a lingering death at forty-five. In *The Fall*, Camus' Jean-Baptiste Clamence retires from Paris to Amsterdam and muses ironically on his success in life. He enjoys his professional success, his standing, and his success with women. Ivan has done all that might be expected of anyone, and yet to no avail. His life amounts to being simply inauthentic and quickly forgotten; he is easy to replace. Jean-Baptiste is not outwardly a failure at all, yet examines himself and confesses to myriad acts of inauthenticity. We might say that both have lived a lie. Yet millions still aspire to such career successes and so-called respectability, and presumably some of them are happy with what they achieve, find love, and do not die with a sense of being mystified.

Let us not ignore that phenomenon whereby failure is romanticized or ironically converted into its opposite. In fashion we can see hobo-chic, for example expensive designer jeans manufactured to look attractively old and torn. Much of the successful career of Charlie Chaplin, who became extremely rich, rested on his portrayal of tramps, for which he was much loved. The English novelist Walter Greenwood was a clerk in a textile firm in Salford. His *Love on the Dole*, published in 1933, in times of great poverty, became a best-seller that some compared with Dostoevsky and many saw as an indictment of failed capitalism. Greenwood's novel was successful in the USA and also became a play, and he was awkwardly propelled into fame and wealth. I recall reading it with great approval during a period when I was young, unemployed, depressed and without love.

Partly echoing early Greek Cynics but also inspired by Zen Buddhism and existentialism, the beatniks of the 1950s included beat poets, novelists, artists and musicians who rejected bourgeois society and its aims. Influenced by French poets and dramatists such as Antonin Artaud and Arthur Rimbaud, and also Americans such as Ralph Waldo Emerson, Henry David Thoreau and Walt Whitman, writers such as William S. Burroughs, Allen Ginsberg and

Jack Kerouac adopted a style in their art, dress and behaviour that conspicuously rejected mainstream norms of the time and place. The beats were seen as beat, beaten down, tired, but also as upbeat and beatific. Ginsberg's famous poem "Howl" begins with the line "I saw the best minds of my generation destroyed by madness". Regarded as failed citizens, disloyal to the American dream of materialism and progress, they saw society as failing real human needs. The beats may be seen as forerunners of hippies, punks and later anarchists and anti-capitalists who continue to regard mainstream society as flawed beyond redemption. Philosophers like Marcuse, critiquing the alienating "one-dimensional society" in the early 1960s, argued that "'Romantic' is a term of condescending defamation which is easily applied to disparaging avant-garde positions, just as the term 'decadent' far more often denounces the genuinely progressive traits of a dying culture than the real factors of decay" (1991: 63). Again we see the problem of determining who is at fault, the dissenting individual (or movement) or mainstream society, perhaps with the only possible answer being both and neither.

In the 1980s, in his poem "My Non-ambitious Ambition", the rebel-rousing, hard-drinking writer Charles Bukowski complains about his discouraging father (who regularly referred to him as a bum): "and I thought, if being a bum is to be the/opposite of what this son-of-a-bitch/is, then that's what I'm going to/ be". He goes on to say "how beautifully I've succeeded". Trite though it is to observe, many reject the model of success presented by parents and feel compelled to assert their own personality even if this means sabotaging the bourgeois success that awaits them. Interestingly, this kind of "script" is often regarded by some psychotherapists as unhealthily rigid, at least for the individual trapped in his or her own early protest against parental oppression.

Philip Roth's *The Humbling* tells the story of a distinguished American classical actor who in his early sixties has "lost his magic"; "the terrible thing happened: he couldn't act ... Instead of the certainty that he was going to be wonderful, he knew he was going to fail" (all this on the very first page). Simon Axler has lost it, he becomes depressed, is afraid he might kill himself and checks into a psychiatric facility. He then goes to live alone (his marriage ended), seemingly accepting his fate. But his new resigned existence is interrupted by a much younger woman with whom he begins an intense relationship, and his outlook brightens in many ways. But when she leaves him he plunges once more, and this time fatally, into despair leading to his shooting himself. After some contemplation he had decided that "the failures were his, as was the bewildering biography on which he was impaled". Roth's terse tragedy offers no particular lesson but it does uncomfortably remind us that even decades of success do not guarantee continuing success and happiness. Axler is well off, has enjoyed celebrity and achievement but cannot accept the loss of his talent, and love, in later life.

Roth's novel is not exactly self-referential and he is a good, imaginative storyteller generally, but his hero is an actor, a fellow artist. Many novelists are castigated for writing novels about middle-class novelists because they have lost touch with ordinary life and live sequestered from the experiences of everyday struggle. The early successes of some writers can lead entropically to later works that lack the earlier energy and originality. This might remind us of academics in so-called ivory towers, whose theories become ever more remote from the subjects they initially set out to understand and communicate. Perhaps it remains an open question whether it is "good for" artists and their audiences to be so divided, and whether it is inevitable that artists are part of a talented elite entertaining and educating the less talented.

Of the visual arts, Lisa Le Feuvre, who draws on Kierkegaard and Ricoeur among other philosophers, says:

Failure ... takes us beyond assumptions and what we think we know. Artists have long turned their attention to the

unrealizability of the quest for perfection, or the open-
endedness of experiment, using both dissatisfaction and
error as means to rethink how we understand our place in
the world. (2010: 12)

Her book contains numerous examples of artists actually courting
and celebrating failure, partly as a route to serendipitous discovery
and partly to subvert conventional views of success. As in Keats's
notion of "negative capability" we are reminded that doubt, uncertainty and unknowing are key aspects of art and life. Replication
of the same old beautiful themes is what art perhaps once was
but creativity means that new perspectives, methods and direc-
tions are always necessary. Interestingly, what is celebrated today
as successful modern art would have been considered ugly, down-
right aesthetic failures two hundred years ago.

Philosophers such as Bernard Williams, dwelling on the theme
of moral luck, often focus on artists such as Paul Gauguin as examples. Gauguin left his wife and children in France to pursue his
artistic aspirations in Tahiti. As it turned out (luckily), he became a
highly successful artist and therefore in retrospect he is perceived
as having redeemed his otherwise irresponsible actions. But if he
had failed in his artistic bid, he might well have been perceived as
a moral failure. We might say that moral luck and ill luck dog the
lives of many artists and writers. Gaugin's friend Vincent van Gogh
achieved little success in his own lifetime and experienced much
suffering, yet became posthumously highly successful: or rather his
work did. Van Gogh's *Still Life: Vase with Fifteen Sunflowers* sold
in 1987 for a record £24.7 million and all his paintings now attract
vast sums.

It was in the context of success and failure that John Berger
(1965) examined the career of Pablo Picasso. Picasso was probably
the twentieth century's best known artist. Unlike van Gogh and
many other artists he did not suffer or die in poverty or obscurity.

He seemed to embody the artistic genius, frequently changing subjects and styles in a lifelong prolific output. Berger suggests that Picasso was a noble savage and bourgeois revolutionary, torn between a bohemian and Marxist temperament and sympathies, and yet catapulted into great commercial success. His millionaire lifestyle gradually sealed him off from raw new experiences and had a negative effect on his art. However prolific and inventive he remained, he became a parody of himself. In many of his later paintings Berger sees evidence of Picasso including self-references, for example to a monkey mocking an old man near a beautiful woman. Picasso seemed the lifelong virile hero of art and life but was aware in such paintings that he was in fact an old man and somewhat ridiculous. If the artist is by calling an outsider and anarchist, then the successful artist, particularly the rich artist, is an object of suspicion. It is on just this point that financial speculation on the art market has raised serious doubts about today's artistic values.

We say that everyone has a novel inside them. It is true that each of us has a slightly different story to tell. But each of us, aside from our prosaic external events, harbours an unexercised hero, murderer, adventurer, rapist, suicide, great lover, martyr, or some combination of these. However, those who fan the aspirations of the not very talented masses by encouraging the common ambition to become a novelist, actor, entertainer, sportsperson (and, these days, counsellor) are surely acting irresponsibly. Very few people can make it in these professions; the failure rate is high, employment scarce and the competition frankly ridiculous. Such aspirations chime with the sentiment that everyone can be famous for fifteen minutes, or be "famous for being famous", as in the case of vacuous celebrities. Yet the fantasy is an important element in capitalist societies, in which people must have constant hope of success with which to motivate themselves. It is also an important hope for the most oppressed and disadvantaged, yet at the same time it is clearly logically faulty. While Barack Obama became the first black president of the USA, the overwhelming majority of poor black and white citizens will never attain any significant power at all.

Another interesting side of the failed novelist or actor scenario is this. Publishing is a commercial enterprise and publishing staff are professionals. Bombarded with the scripts of new novels by aspiring novelists, publishers make rapid but presumably skilled decisions and reject most of these, identifying the few that show real promise. However, as we know, this often isn't true. Books that turn out to be runaway bestsellers have quite often been rejected earlier by other publishers. These include *Jonathan Livingston Seagull*, *Kon-Tiki*, *Dubliners*, *Zen and the Art of Motorcycle Maintenance*, *We Need to Talk about Kevin*, *Lorna Doone*, *Gone with the Wind* and, of course, *Harry Potter and the Philosopher's Stone*. A certain element of randomness rules in the world of commerce. It is a fantasy, and flimsy logic, to imagine that talent will always win out. It is not only goodness that is fragile but natural justice too.

One of the saddest examples is the novel *A Confederacy of Dunces* by John Kennedy Toole, who committed suicide, partly due to the failure to get his book published. His mother subsequently promoted it, it was published in 1980, has been critically acclaimed and won the Pulitzer Prize. Much more common are countless examples of books that fail to sell many copies, sometimes regardless of how good they are, the market being fickle. This is true of theatre and film too, where box-office successes may be "critical failures" and vice versa.

Our human characteristics include a vigilant consciousness, a constant awareness of fragility and entropy, and seeking meanings, solutions or distractions. We might see religion, the arts, media, sport, entertainment, travel and tourism, the internet, fashion and general consumerism as part of the same complex of psychologically needed myths and stimuli. None of these are vital in the sense that securing food, housing, companionship, sex and safety is vital. But they do appear to be emotionally vital in so far as we need emotional symbols, assurances, soothing and catharsis. However, they are all in the subjective domain and they appeal to the masses in a way that science does not. Bookshops are full of fiction and non-fiction, as if fiction is primary, and book sales reflect this. Television too reflects some need for substantial distraction, and the small screen has carried across to the pervasive world of the internet.

In addition to the mass popularity of literature, we have an industry of literary criticism, also based essentially on subjectivity. All of us are amateur critics of the arts and media. I read or half-read some novels and think that they fail to engage me, or they don't speak to me. I may sometimes condemn them as rubbish. But when something is hailed by critics and endorsed by sales or viewing figures as brilliant, I may pause to think that if I don't "get it" I may be a failure as an aesthetic judge. Indeed, I am not interested in most sports, or conceptual art or opera, or religion, and I wonder if this is a flaw or limitation of mine. However, we can see in certain examples that subjective judgements prevail here. In many religions the media, dance and frivolity are regarded as sinful. Philosophers disagree over the meaning and value of the arts, Plato being famously sceptical about their worth but Aristotle dwelling quite a bit on aesthetics in his *Poetics*. There is also considerable debate about the merits of so-called high art versus trashy media arts, about the spiritually uplifting nature of art versus its opiate effects, and about the status of the artist as genius or mad. John Carey's *What Good are the Arts?* works through such issues, reminding us that Sartre, for one, "puts the case that the literature of the past is irrelevant, dead, and only for losers" (2005: 175).

It may be my aesthetic or emotional failing (or simply my subjective bent) not to appreciate much the art gallery, theatre, sports stadium or church. But certainly some films, books and music can move me emotionally and edge me into new insights, and television and other ephemeral media can distract and inform me.

Where I believe the arts fail us is in luring us into transient states of emotional and aesthetic uplift that we then take to be the heights of true experience. In other words, the aesthetic and emotional become symbolic substitutes for enlightenment, for penetrating our false and troublesome human consciousness. The arts complex joins religion, politics, psychotherapy, indeed all institutions, in losing its original inspiration via gradual corruption. It is a tragedy that so often the best minds of our species – Socrates, Aristotle, Jesus, the Buddha, Shakespeare, Picasso and many others – leave a legacy of misunderstanding, imitation and institutionalization, or rather that we fail to grasp and embody their insights. Even sadder is the possibility that the vast majority of us are so immersed in our sedimented false consciousness that we shall never be liberated from it.

In his somewhat bleak but seminal book *Very Little … Almost Nothing*, Critchley agrees that "it is no longer clear *what* counts as a work of art and *how* a work counts" (1997: 154) and quotes from Beckett's *Molloy* the phrase "a form fading among fading forms". For Critchley, Beckett's work resists and partly mocks philosophical analysis, and yet philosophers such as himself, Theodor W. Adorno and Stanley Cavell find Beckett highly inspiring. Critchley wants to assert that in Beckett we find not the meaninglessness of existence but a successful portrayal of modern human confrontation with meaning. Literature is, in Beckett's words, "a long sin against silence" (quoted in *ibid.*: 167).

Chris Waitts's film *A Complete History of my Sexual Failures* (2008) is a documentary of his own failed relationships, portraying him as a hapless, deadpan, almost schizoid character. He probes for possible reasons for his failures (immaturity, self-absorption, lack of commitment, chaotic behaviour, impotence, etc.) until he realizes *emotionally* on talking with his most loved ex-girlfriend that he has failed to appreciate his opportunities. At that point he fortuitously meets a new woman, wacky like him, and failure looks at last like turning to possible happiness. This is one of those funny (to some) but also very sad films suggesting that a sustained honest encounter with one's own emotional failings may yield real insights. I found myself crying at the end of it, as I did when I read Roth's *Everyman* and Sebastian Faulks's *Human Traces*. Different stories and their treatments touch each of us differently but we might wonder at our common susceptibility to being moved and influenced much more by spiritual and artistic phenomena than by difficult scientific and philosophical texts.

The critically successful film *Magnolia* (1999) portrays a number of interwoven scenarios – including child sex abuse, marital strife, undue parental pressure on a child, extreme misogyny – that demand emotional and ethical reactions from viewers. Mike Leigh's realist films similarly demand a reaction. In *Another Year* (2010) the action takes place around a comfortably off, slightly smug middle-aged couple (she is a counsellor). By contrast Ken is a sad drunk, Mary is an all-round failure who also drinks to excess, and Ronnie is an expressionless, inarticulate widower. Superficially they are all friends, but over an excruciating dinner we can see that Ronnie's and Mary's losers' worlds are far away from the successful world of the middle-class, happily married, graduate couple (and their professional son and his girlfriend). It's difficult to decide whether mere moral luck, education and class separate them or if Mary in particular has unskilfully or wilfully fucked her life up in contrast to the virtuous couple. In Lars von Trier's *Breaking the Waves* (1996), however, it is easy to see the lead character Bess as a beautifully innocent martyr to the cold and wicked moralism of Scottish clergy and peers. The causes of global catastrophe are unknown in the film *The Road* (2009, adapted from Cormac McCarthy's novel) but utterly bleak failure including cannibalism impinges on all, with the protective father and his son hopefully and fallibly "carrying the fire" for civilized human values.

Many films have effectively shown that systemic social failures (slavery, sexism, racism) can be, have been and need to be opposed, and those kept in failure positions need to become aspirational, not to endlessly bemoan their fate of being held in a failure position by their oppressors. This is broadly true of films as various as *Spartacus, One Flew Over the Cuckoo's Nest, Educating Rita, Freedom Writers* and *Slumdog Millionaire*. In the genre of popular catastrophe movie, *The Towering Inferno* indicted the failure of builders to adhere to regulations for high-quality materials and *The Day After Tomorrow* showed prophetically that failure to heed early warnings of climate change may lead to large-scale disaster and human deaths.

Many of the examples of failure given in this book are about men and by men. As a small adjustment, consider briefly Meredith Broussard's *The Dictionary of Failed Relationships* (2003). Written by twenty-six contemporary young female writers, this book amusingly and sometimes painfully covers a wide range of relationship failures, reminding us just how common these are, especially in our early years of hope, flirting and courtship. Fantasy, misjudgements and outright mismatches, clumsy gropings, violence and more: this is the stuff of failed couplings, much of it even well before the chronically tedious marriage or bitter divorce.

While failure is usually portrayed in dark terms, it also has a lighter side. Indeed, failure is at the very core of slapstick comedy. Things going visibly wrong, people falling over, getting hit and run over are the ingredients of much silent film but also of a great deal of contemporary comedy. Social failure, *faux pas*, domestic farce: these all form the contents of much film and many television programmes. So-called reality television permits us to look closely at personal failings, interpersonal clumsiness and failed social skills, and many seem fascinated by the spectacle. Popular, loved American comics, such as those by Harvey Pekar and Robert Crumb, show vivid autobiographical failures with work, health and relationships: the graphic counterpoint to the glossy American dream.

Or take a cartoon book such as *You are Worthless*, which might read as a dangerous incitement to self-hatred but is very funny as it draws on satire of the self-help industry and on negative probability:

> Try another role-model exercise: Picture someone you look up to who is very rich, good-looking, successful, and loved by everyone. Now slowly count to one million, because that's how many years in which you will never be as rich, good-looking, successful, or loved as that person.
>
> (Pratt & Dikkers 1999: 6)

So, the arts and media frequently chart our failures. They demonstrate that human existence is shot through with tragic events, unpredictable and uncontrollable forces and often absurd situations. Artists and writers themselves often remain economic failures, except for the lucky few who sometimes deservedly and sometimes by fluke or absurdity or capitalist distortion become rich celebrities. The arts reflect the human condition but perhaps, as Plato argued, they also fail us. There is melancholy in the intuition that lives do not end happily ever after, as in some novels, and that many lives are low-level tragicomedies. There is also an important, underdeveloped critique of art in the likes of Bertolt Brecht's anti-individualist drama and poetry: for all its aesthetic striving and anarchistic posing, most art is arguably a political failure.

5. Being a failure

In Chapter 2 we looked at how individuals may fail across the lifespan. Here the emphasis is on how fallibility, flaws and failings can add up to an experience or perception of enormous, almost embodied failure: *being a failure*. Three features of the phrase "being a failure" should readily jump out at us. The first is that we undeniably have such a self-concept in our culture, as in the sad statement "I am a complete failure", which some people make, often with variable accompanying adjectives such as total, abject or miserable. The second is that we may readily accept responsibility for personal failure even when the obvious elements of biological and social failure are quite outside our making or control. The third is that it seems unlikely, if not impossible, for anyone actually to *be* a (total) failure, in a similar way to being itself not being non-being. Any of us may fail at certain things but none us can be a perfect failure.

In his survey of philosophical views on "status anxiety", Alain de Botton acknowledges:

The fear of failing at tasks would perhaps not be so great were it not for an awareness of how often failure tends to be harshly viewed and interpreted by others. Fear of the material consequences of failure is compounded by fear of the unsympathetic attitude of the world towards failure, of its haunting proclivity to refer to those who have failed as "losers" – a word callously signifying both that people have lost and that

they have at the same time forfeited any right to sympathy for
having done so.   (2004: 157)

Returning to my own example in the introduction to this book,
I have to concede that in conventional terms of occupational status
I have had some success. Regarding my health, well-being and
contentment, I cannot fairly describe myself as a failure. If we take
the Socratic criterion of the examined life, I am more a success
than a failure. But I am past my heyday; redundancy combined
with ageing carries some associative sting of being on or closer to
the scrapheap, uncomfortably close to the status of has-been. But
with regard to certain aspects of my life, there are more cutting
and longer-lasting nuances of failure. As a child I had to take part
in sports at school, yet no matter how hard I tried in any athletic or
other sporting event I always came last or somewhere near the end.
I learned early on that I was "no good at" these things and probably never would be. In addition, it became clear that I could not
grasp maths or science subjects after about the age of eleven, nor
did I have much practical ability. None of this has changed across
my life. In some ways I have excelled intellectually in an arts and
humanities direction commensurately with failing in other direc-
tions. Perhaps one can choose not to measure oneself by the criterion of "all-rounder" and instead be self-accepting with regard to
actual strengths.

In at least one important way, as time goes by I fail more often
or habitually; I mean in the domain of technology, particularly
computer use. Although I regularly use a laptop and indeed depend
on it, I encounter frequent IT problems that thwart me and are
associated with frustration and unhappiness. We could put it this
way: that I fail to adapt to an increasingly technological society. This
may sound trivial and to some it appears unbelievable or "defeatist",
but I stand in relation to technology where dyslexics stand in relation to literacy. I find idiosyncratic and cumbersome ways around

IT and other technological problems but I will never be "much good" (competent) in this domain. It *is* a problem in so far as it has become an inescapable part of daily life for most of us, whereas I am not obliged to play, nor am I pressurized into playing, sports (or participating in dancing, drama and so on). It is also an aspect of life in which others freely tease – as in "You're a dinosaur" or "You're a technophobe" (which has connotations of nuisance, Luddite, creator of your own problems, etc.) – in a manner that in other domains might be called bullying and disrespectful labelling.

If we take relational endurance or marital continuity as a criterion of success, then in this domain too I have not yet been an obvious success story. However, I am persistent here; relationships matter much more to me than IT does, so I would not call myself a failure. Overall, I might say that I have made the most of the hand of cards dealt me; I have navigated my way around my maternally derived relational fault line, instinctively playing to my advantages and talents and not beating myself up *too* much about my failures. However, many individuals regard themselves as failures and/or are perceived to be failures, or even a "waste of space", or the objects of other belittling terminology. We might say that some are born failures, some achieve failure, and some have failure thrust upon them. It is certainly the case that many are born at the bottom of the social pecking order and remain there. Arguably it is far harder to ascend to success from a low baseline than to fall or fail from a position of privilege. People can move in either direction, however, and we may note the common attitudes of downward snobbery and upward envy. Each of us is in principle free to ignore conventional social markers of success and to define ourselves by our own subjective criteria regardless of outward achievements, but this is not easy, requiring resources of self-esteem and tough reasoning that not all possess. Some of us can take comfort from Diogenes' example of self-determination and rejection of social coercion, and some can possibly emulate him, but relatively few appear to do this.

So, who is "a failure" or "loser"? We have seen some examples in the previous chapter. Consider a personal statement by a nineteen-year-old man feeling suicidal:

> 19 and a virgin … I will never get laid … can't do anything right … I was one of the biggest losers in my High School … Girls would laugh at me … I am short, ugly, … I have no skills, abilities, or talents. I am worthless … Deep down I know that I am a failure and destined to die alone and miserable.
>
> (Alejandro 2007)

This painful account contains a mixture of presumed facts and flawed reasoning. Presumably this young man actually is a virgin and short, he may have performed poorly at school, and he may well have been laughed at and bullied. It would not be surprising for someone in this position to feel depressed and even suicidal. Like it or not, taller males are usually preferred over short ones. Talented and attractive people have been shown to have better life chances and material rewards than others. To some extent this nineteen-year-old man has grasped some of life's cruel realities. He also shows a great deal of honesty. Many of us struggle against such feelings by pretending to ourselves and others to be fine.

It is fairly clear where he is incorrect (without wishing to add to his heavy list of negatives). Quite probably, one day he will get laid, he almost certainly does do some things right, does have some skills and abilities he doesn't recognize, and cannot know that he will die alone and miserable (although he may). He certainly *feels* this bad subjectively. But we would be able to find young people fitting this description whose lives turned out well enough later on. In other words, even many short, ugly, bullied and unhappy people eventually have somewhat decent relationships, overcome their inner distress, resist suicidal thoughts and live somewhat contented lives. We could also point to the lives of people who face much worse adversities than this and overcome them. But it does not follow that if many do turn such misery into a degree of success, he himself can or must. He may not have the natural resilience, the fight, that others have; or he may simply decide that it isn't worth the fight for the sake of the few positive returns he may obtain.

He may feel no obligation to any moral argument against suicide, perhaps instinctively realising, as Benatar (2006) claims to demonstrate, that human existence is invariably more painful than pleasurable. Perhaps this example also shows that most of us are conditioned not to accept accounts of failure and suicidal wishes without putting up a pro-life, optimistic argument. In other words, few of us are likely to agree with his reasoning or intentions, or even to keep an open mind about these matters: an interpretation of one's life as a failure pointing to the desirability of suicide seems anathema to most (but not all) of us. This might suggest that a profound sense of potential failure, or simply the prescience of our own inescapable death, sits inside all of us, demanding fierce denial. Long before Freud formulated his views on the "death instinct", Socrates had spoken of philosophy as a lifelong preparation for death (Desmond 1988).

In my view the poorest kinds of argument against a position such as this young man's are (i) the "stop feeling sorry for yourself" kind and (ii) the denial kind. The first kind brings us back to the linked questions of rationality, free agency or volition, and the problem of *akrasia*: why can't this young man simply put his bad memories and negative predictions behind him, see his present choices clearly, and start a programme to enhance positive behaviours that will improve his life chances? (Indeed, why can't we all freely and sensibly do this?) The second kind argues thus: "You're not so short, ugliness is all in the mind, lots of girls would fancy you if you gave them the chance, …". The first one at least has the merit of examining options, and potentially generating hope and new planning strategies, while the second is challenging but logically and psychologically flimsy.

Perhaps those freakishly perfection-approaching specimens of optimal beauty, intelligence, charm, wealth, fitness and health set the bar high for success and leave the rest of us dimly aware of our comparative failures. And perhaps in sheer, unfair statistical terms, there are those who are truly the obverse of the above: ugly, unintelligent, hard to like, poor, unfit or infirm. Socrates, famously ugly himself, in dialogue with Critobulus was said to have argued for the superiority of ugly facial features, and certainly seemed not to suffer any low self-esteem due to his own. But then he did possess a superior intellect and high status. And Sartre, renowned for his ugliness (he was very short, half-blind and had bad teeth), almost took pride in his indifference to his body while nevertheless attracting many women.

Social animals do not have the language to refer to each other as failures or to internalize such self-concepts. Nonetheless, it is often abundantly clear who is the alpha male, who has mating rights, and priority for food. In some cases smaller mammals have been said to resort to trickery and rape in order to get what they want. It may or may not seem feasible to present this phenomenon as grounds for supporting the proposition that failure is an intrinsic part of all life. My viability is necessarily tied together with my fallibility. If I am low in any hierarchy I may face increased threats to my reproductive prospects and to my very life. I either have to submit to the conditions of my social order or find ways of compensating for my lowly position, whether by deception, making myself useful and subservient, finding allies or other strategies; and my tactics and risk-taking may backfire. This seems to hold true for many animals as well as human beings.

We can certainly draw on the argument that we are all successful, since we have been born and survived the challenges of birth, illnesses and accidents. Theologically we can say that each of us is equally precious in the sight of God. A common default position in a great deal of philosophy is the assumption of universal and equally distributed rationality. That is, if anything can be demonstrated to be objectively logical then it applies to all human beings, and all should be equally able to implement its conclusions. In other words, we are all or should be rational agents limited only by the degree of our willingness to live virtuously. Of course, not all philosophers share this view. For example, Jonathan Jacobs argues that "we typically regard ethical failures as failures to uphold standards grounded in principles or criteria that are (at least to some extent) understood and acknowledged by the agents who have acted badly ... But not everyone is ethically capable" (2001: 35). Being ethically disabled by delusion or cognitive impairment is what Jacobs has in mind. But arguably a spectrum of ethical ability exists, some possessing innate strong will and others being weak-willed and/or impaired by subtle addictions, obesity, deficits of empathy and so on.

Of course, there are many examples available in literature, anecdotally and online, of people who have fallen from grace but picked themselves up, dusted themselves off and started all over again; or those who have hauled themselves from nowhere and overcome huge obstacles to become successful, rich and famous. A fair amount of literature describes such narratives and their lessons, for example Steve Young's popular *Great Failures of the Extremely Successful* (2002). What we comment on rather less are those whose success is so entwined with their status and hubris that even when they display spectacular moral failings sometimes causing misery around themselves (I am thinking of Tony Blair, vastly overpaid bankers of the early 2000s, and their like) they seem to escape the epithet of failure.

This is all part and parcel of the American dream. It is the view of Sandage (2005) that the term "I feel like a failure" was not used in the personal sense until around 1860 and then it was as a direct result of bankruptcies and economic failures stemming from the surge of American commercial activities. In Sandage's detailed historical account, credit reports, police records and school grades share responsibility for the construction of the distinctive sense of personal failure. I doubt that this is true beyond the specific modern connotations of the word "failure", since the sentiment "I am a miserable sinner" has a much longer history (with etymological origins in the Middle Ages) and a quite similar internalized and globalized negative meaning. Indeed, the New Testament warns in Revelations 21:21 that the Lamb's Book of Life records clearly who is to be denied entry to eternity through the Pearly Gates on their physical death, and part of one's worthiness relates to how well or otherwise one has used one's God-given "talents" in life (Matthew 25:14–30). This latter parable has been variously, and usually erroneously, interpreted as fulfilling one's human potential and investing one's capital wisely. Consider too Matthew 5:48 – "Be therefore perfect, even as your Father which is in Heaven is perfect" – and its moral and psychological impact on anxiously flawed humans. Either way, many of us may at least unconsciously fear that we may appear negatively in the heavenly ledger or indeed in the Big Red Book of Dun and Bradstreet credit reports, not to mention failing job interviews constructed around psychological profile tests.

Pause here to consider the case of Kierkegaard, the Danish philosopher strongly influenced by Socrates' writings, who experienced considerable ridicule, rejection, criticism and anguish in his own time, yet came to be credited as a major thinker who challenged the Hegelian tradition of depersonalized philosophy and theology. Kierkegaard promoted responsibility for the self, for accepting the despair inherent in this life, and for choosing one's beliefs and behaviour as an individual. This entailed for him a single life and an isolated anti-Church stance. He died at forty-two. Standing at his grave in Copenhagen, I pondered his words, translated for me, which included the hopes that strife would now be completely gone and he would spend all his time talking to Jesus. I felt overcome by sadness for this poor man and wondered if it was fair of me 156 years later, in an ethos of atheism and psychoanalysis, to regard him as having suffered from some unfortunate psychopathology and having been deluded in his views. I feel certain that he did not pass through any pearly gates or hold any talks with Jesus, and am pretty sure that this "father of existentialism" had a somewhat failed life that he compensated for with clever but deeply flawed writing. And I know that I lay myself open to charges of certain forms of arrogance and intellectual error in doing so. But how can we know whose insights and philosophies to trust?

Are there ways in which we can clearly categorize people as failures and begin to locate the sources of our judgements? As we saw in Chapter 2, there are probably key moments for failure to emerge. Significantly poor performances in school can, and often do, lead to compound failure: the student is perceived as failing across time, across subjects and perhaps as showing no signs of being capable of any real success. Some schools and teachers may bend over backwards to avoid such stigmatizing, or they may seek out at least some small areas for praise and improvement, but many individuals still leave school feeling like failures. My own father, who attended an English school in the 1920s, certainly carried around with him for a lifetime the belief that he was an "idiot" because he could not grasp what was required of him and could not perform well in exams. Even when he became an established master plasterer and worked on prestigious projects at Buckingham Palace and elsewhere, this feeling never left him. It remains true today that the manually skilful are often considered inferior to the academically and professionally successful, regardless of their true contribution to society.

Although we now like to point punitively to "failing schools", schools do not really carry any stigma across their lives. A small proportion of teachers are dismissed for incompetence. But it's likely that large numbers of young people leaving school every year have learnt they are failures or relative failures. The sociologist Pierre Bourdieu's intensive study of the French socially neglected underclass (or "subproletariat") makes this point bitingly:

> The feeling of being tied to a degrading ("rotten") place by lack
> of money and transportation and doomed to a degradation
> (and to degradations) that weighs on them like a curse, or,
> more simply, a stigmata that blocks access to work, to leisure
> activities, and to consumer goods, etc.; and, more profoundly,
> the inexorably repeated experience of failure, first in school,
> then in the labor market, which prevents or discourages any
> reasonable hope for the future. (1999: 185)

Such institutionalized failures are far from new but there is often scant political will or success in transforming them. Meanwhile, school pupils in these situations learn that they are abandoned and devalued and create their own responses, often angry and violent ones.

Of those who are relatively successful in any school system, they must also be aware where their grades and their choice and level of subject and college or university place them. Indeed I know mature adults who lament that they "only went to X University" and "only got a 2:2". Saddest of all are those with high aspirations who, failing to get into the prestigious university of their choice, or failing to gain high enough grades, commit suicide. Now, we might easily claim that education is the site of considerable failure creation and aim to reform education itself but, as Bourdieu and others have repeatedly shown, it is easier to allow victims to continue in failure than to make genuine changes at the macro-level.

While religion often presents the case that each of us is unique and precious in the sight of God, the downside of religion for individuals is fairly clear: if you fail to accept the terms of most religions you may be regarded as a sinner or infidel and be banished from heaven or paradise for all eternity, as if punishment in this life is insufficient. Even if you are religious you may suffer from the terrible feeling of guilt that you will never be good enough, you will never be saved, and God can see beyond your outwardly religious compliance into your rotten hypocritical soul. Such negative sentiments probably drive the behaviour of ascetics who deny themselves pleasure, flagellate and in other ways punish themselves. Not all religions or all individual religious experiences are of this negative nature. But all religions have positive images of prophets and saviours (and contrasting stories of evil and heretical characters) and it is small wonder if, in the face of these, many feel like failures. I have not achieved anything like the enlightened insight of the Buddha, nor the heroic self-sacrifice of Jesus Christ (nor anything like the tormented but celebrated Kierkegaard's contribution). Nor, in the domain of philosophy, can many of us match the powers of reasoning and heroic self-sacrifice of Socrates or the readiness of Diogenes to spurn worldly comfort and status. In all such moral hierarchies, most of us are perhaps miserable failures.

In the domain of psychotherapy, many of us can be counted as failures in terms of our neuroses or pathologies as we suffer from a panoply of depressions, anxieties, sexual and other personal problems. Most of us have not wrestled successfully with our demons in the reportedly heroic and insightful manner of Freud and Jung or the lead characters in the dramatically successful case studies of some psychotherapists. Many of us deny that we have such problems or dimly perceive that we have but are too fearful to seek therapy. Some who enter therapy still remain neurotic – the double failure, as in religion, of seeking salvation or cure but failing to find it or benefit from it: ten years of psychoanalysis, say, and "still as fucked up as ever". In my own case (and many others'), expensive immersion in Janov's primal therapy (touted as "*the* cure for neurosis") in the 1970s would have to be considered a failure, or double failure, of this kind, unless, of course, we point the finger of failure at the therapy and its originator. Or perhaps in some cases it is both the needy person and the supplier of hope who are moral and neurotic failures.

Albert Ellis, the late American psychotherapist who created rational emotive behaviour therapy (REBT), took particular exception to the ways in which we rate ourselves as failures. In his *The Myth of Self-Esteem* (2005) he repeats his message that if we want a reasonably happy life we had better learn to accept ourselves with all our failings. We may recognize those of our behaviours that are undesirable but we are wise not to condemn ourselves as persons. He uses the term "unconditional self-acceptance" (USA, a nice undermining of the American obsession with success) to underpin the idea that we are worthy as persons regardless of our actions and our fallibility. Ellis has been highly critical of perfectionism as a common driver of unhappiness, since perfectionism by its nature demands standards of excellence in all spheres that must sooner or later prove unachievable. Ellis is of particular relevance here because he has always insisted that his ideas are derived from Epictetus' Stoicism. In *The Myth of Self-Esteem*, he specifically alludes to a number of philosophers and theologians who have stimulated or informed the creation of his REBT concepts, including Martin Buber, Heidegger, Kierkegaard, Lao Tzu, Sartre, Baruch Spinoza and Paul Tillich. Suggesting that the obsession with self-esteem (or "not being a success") is a sickness, Ellis heavily promotes the view that self-acceptance and anti-perfectionism are roads to better mental health and happiness.

Fear of failure haunts many, including those who attempt to hide the fear. There is the woman who, feeling a failure, marries a man she does not love so that she can have married ("successful") status; and her marriage soon fails. There are many who suffer from imaginary failure, especially those with obsessive-compulsive disorder who imagine they have left taps and switches on or hurt people. It's likely that some highly successful intellectuals, such as Wittgenstein, can be considered to fit the profile for Asperger's Syndrome: as socially unresponsive as they are talented in their own specialisms. It has been well documented that many suffering from bipolar disorder (previously manic-depressive disorder) are high risk-takers and a significant portion of these enter business professions. The energy and elation of the entrepreneurial bipolar personality may lead to great successes in the short to medium term but non-medicated or uncontrolled manic flights are quite likely to cause boom and bust effects in the long term. A friend of mine went from moderately successful management positions to a wealth-generating property business only to crash to poverty in later life via divorces, alcoholism, anger problems and hospitalization. Among those celebrities reckoned probably to have suffered from bipolar disorder are Vincent van Gogh, Kurt Cobain, Stephen Fry, Mel Gibson, Ernest Hemingway, Spike Milligan and Jackson Pollock. Highly creative risk-takers are likely to contribute to business and arts successes disproportionately but also to experience disproportionate failure and, often, mental illness and suicide. This is contentious territory that rightfully attracts the attention of the philosophy of mind (Graham 2010).

We might also consider anomalous cases. Take, for example, Howard Hughes, the American billionaire. Enormously gifted, Hughes was an industrialist, engineer, aviator, film producer and director who broke several air-speed records, designed aircraft, developed the company Trans World Airlines, married and was associated with Hollywood stars and wielded political influence. From about his thirties he developed severe mental health problems, chiefly obsessive-compulsive disorder, which led to a reclusive and eccentric lifestyle living in hotels, having dietary and contamination obsessions, urinating in bottles and becoming extremely unkempt. In chronic pain and on multiple medications, Hughes finally died of kidney failure. By many standards Hughes, one of the world's richest men, could never be classified as a failure. One could reasonably assume, however, that his bizarre behaviour and many interpersonal conflicts were accompanied by great subjective distress and he would probably not be nominated for many all-round successful human being awards. This example brings up questions of whether a balanced life is necessarily better than an unbalanced one, that is, whether outward success and inner happiness combined is a superior formula to, say, genius with outward success but inner distress; and again, who is to judge who is a success or failure?

Controversy and ambiguity still surround the case of Bruce Ismay, owner of the White Star Line, which built the *Titanic*. Ismay was aboard the *Titanic* just before it sank a hundred years ago. He may or may not have urged higher speed but he did find his way into a lifeboat and to safety when 1,500 passengers out of 2,223 died. He is said to be responsible for the decision to limit lifeboats to a much smaller number than the ship's capacity. During subsequent hearings he denied any impropriety or cowardice but many considered him ignominious and the press were unforgiving. At least one writer names him as a "moral failure", links his fate with that of Joseph Conrad's character Lord Jim, but suggests that the guilt he must have lived with is actually not so uncommon, many of us holding a secret sense of letting others down (Wilson 2011).

One could multiply examples similar to that of Howard Hughes. For instance Wittgenstein, as mentioned above, was regarded as a genius of modern philosophy and talented in many other ways, yet he was a troubled and often disliked person. Take Stephen Hawking, wheelchair bound with motor neurone disease for decades yet a leading theoretical physicist: we might speak of him as suffering from a serious biological failure alongside outstanding academic and scientific success. The footballer George Best, for all his sporting and financial success, failed to conquer his alcohol problem and died of it. Eminent politicians such as Bill Clinton and Jesse Jackson have succumbed to extramarital sexual temptations, which may not earn them the epithetic of "failure" so much as "flawed character". We can object that neurological disorders should not be conflated with moral errors or hypocrisies (the former being passive, the latter active) but this distinction would also bring us back to questions about the very nature of tragic flaws.

Let's note in passing too the modern tendency to assume that explanations for personal failures lie more in the domain of psychology and science generally than in philosophy. The psychologist Robert Sternberg's *Why Smart People Can Be So Stupid* (2002), for example, gives a brief mention of Aristotelian *akrasia* but mainly focuses on foolishness and folly that can be framed in psychological terms. The philosopher Janet Radcliffe Richards contrasts two examples thus: (i) "she failed the exam because she didn't want to seem cleverer than her friend" and (ii) "she failed the exam because she wasn't clever enough to pass" (2000: 19). We might see in these examples of psychoanalytic thinking and the psychology of intelligence respectively but Radcliffe Richards designates the first as teleological and the second non-teleological. Like anything else, we can use failure as a means to something if our own priorities differ from those of others. Here, friendship is more important than academic success. We saw the same in the case of the writer Charles Bukowski: the choice to fail for his own ends, to distance himself from his hated father.

There was at least one point in my life when I definitely felt "a failure". I was about twenty and had taken LSD. I was standing in a street in the suburbs of London, staring across the road at a pleasant, affluent-looking house. The husband and father was getting out of his car on returning from work. His attractive wife and children seemed to appear on cue on the doorstep, full of genuine enthusiasm and love. The scene was no doubt magnified by the drug but the intensity of its meaning and rebuke for me couldn't have been sharper: I would never have any of that, I was a loser, a failure through and through. I would never have a career paying a salary that would make me an attractive prospect; I would never have a pretty wife or kids, or a nice house. I was an outsider. I would be lucky to avoid becoming a tramp. I wanted the love and success that this scene represented but I didn't have it in me to grasp any career, to believe in any occupation, and I never would have. I adopted a contemptuous attitude towards mindless adaptation to the capitalist treadmill but deep down I wanted at least some of the goodies, especially the pretty wife. Later I got many of the things in this scene, lost some of them, and even now experience some of the related vicissitudes of desire and disappointment. Love, beauty, contentment: now you have them, now you don't. And who knows what actually happened to the actors in my poignant, LSD-enhanced snapshot?

We cannot talk about contemporary individual failures without also asking questions about failure as socially constructed. Some humans have always been weaker or more vulnerable than others. Many have been exploited as slaves, from the time of ancient Greece and Rome through medieval times to the transatlantic shipping of Africans to America in the sixteenth century and even into our own day. Nietszche accuses us of succumbing to a "slave morality" engendered by Christianity. It is not that humans underwent a Fall, but that we bought into the theology of the Fall, which betrays our true nature, in Nietszche's terms. In some sense we all allow ourselves to be enslaved to a religious morality of meekness instead of accepting and pushing through the pain and violence inherent in life's tragedy. Those who are physically enslaved may have little real choice but most of us have been in thrall to Christian and other religious recommendations of guilt, weakness and altruism: to the superstition that God is watching us like an omnipotent slave-master. Religion – a good deal of it patriarchal in character – has failed us.

Perceptions of some as inferior – even as belonging to a wholly inferior race – underpin slavery, a point that brings us uncomfortably close to acknowledging the gender dimension of failure. Women have been treated as inferior and certainly as exploitable: as domestic slaves in all but name. Paradoxically, it is men who have most commonly received the designation of "failure", however, at least in terms of commerce, sport and other traditionally male domains. Women have been more likely to refer to themselves or been referred to as failures in connection with reproduction, mothering and appearance. Female friends readily tell me that they have always felt like failures on the basis of "not being good looking enough, not having the perfect body". Whole social and ethnic groups have internalized some sense of being failures. You might not be disabled had you not displeased God somehow, and some cultures frankly frown on female babies and dispose of some of them. For *some* gay people, their sexuality feels like a failure, so that a homosexual man may feel like an inferior or "failed man".

Interestingly, philosophers for all their probing of important themes have not been above relegating women to an inferior status. Vigdis Songe-Møller (2002) argues forcibly that from Socrates onwards women have been excluded and vilified, not only being treated as insignificant as thinkers and citizens but as to blame for many of life's problems. In ancient Athens, where democracy was formulated for equals, those equals notably excluded women and slaves. For Plato, Aristotle and most other early philosophers, "man was, as it were, the true human, whereas the woman could only be defined as a negation of the man (Plato) or as a defective man (Aristotle)" (Songe-Møller 2002: 80). What is a defective man if not a failure? What does it mean to be a woman or slave if not an "imperfect version of a man"?

Things have changed somewhat, so that today when "godly humans" are those with great wealth, power and celebrity status, the poor are (perceived as) the failures. Money, not intellect as in ancient Greece and Rome, is *the* defining criterion of success and status. We have no Socrates or Diogenes in our midst. Individually we may have no particularly outstanding flaw, yet through any prevailing sociocultural lens you and I can be designated a failure simply for being black, gay, a woman, disabled and so on, and doubly and trebly so if we fall under two or more of these groups. Factor in the adjectives and phrases fat, short, ugly, old, unhealthy, poor, "not very bright" and similar others, and it is clear just how failure-loaded any person's existence can be. And despite our rational protests to the contrary, we may internalize such judgements to the extent that we find it extremely difficult not to think of ourselves as failures, hopeless failures: abject, worthless persons.

But it can work like this too. I am white, male, heterosexual, not disabled or ugly; I am financially comfortable enough, have some success under my belt and am loved. So what can I authentically know about the wretched state of feeling like a failure and being cast in a failure role, sufficient to write about it and expecting to be taken seriously? In what ways, if any, have I taken on board the moral impact of what I am saying here to the point of doing anything meaningful about it? Most of my time is devoted to self-maintenance and the pursuit of pleasure. In tiny ways I may salve my conscience, for example by giving occasional small amounts to charity and by being warm and kind towards friends and acquaintances. But my own daily existence is quite comfortable. I read that "the income of the world's 358 richest people equals that of the 2.3 billion poorest" and I am aware that my middle-range comfort is the flipside of the discomfort of billions who are out of sight, powerless and exploited (Farmer 2005). These macro-failures of global justice help to sustain my quite moderately successful Western lifestyle, and not only mine but that of millions of my compatriots, even some of whom are relatively oppressed and who feel like failures. To some degree, most of us fail to be affected by shocking facts and figures like that above, and we fail to do anything about it. Let us recall here Descartes' "infinity of errors and imperfections" and Ricoeur's echoing this in the case he makes for human fallibility.

Now, all this leads us into an area I shall refer to simply as semantic perplexity. Failure is a plastic term that can be inserted into almost any discourse to the point where its meaning may be overstretched and lost. We can use it to refer to individuals, institutions, aspects of history and cosmology and its meaning is highly context-sensitive. It can also refer to major events, enduring states or fleeting moments. Following on from the above discussion about individuals as perceived failures and about moral failure, we easily enter into semantic perplexity. I might say I am a moral failure for pretending to care about those commonly perceived as failures, as well as a failure as a human being who does nothing active to alleviate the plight of billions on whom my own success is partly parasitical. (This is my bad faith, a kind of phoney ethical agonizing.) I could then say that thinking along such lines is a cognitive error or pointless exercise resembling the pathological scrupulosity of people afflicted by obsessive-compulsive disorder. In fact I am inclined to claim that we are all failures as human beings who share in sustaining a grossly unjust world, and further that we attempt to hide these failures behind weaselly linguistic pseudo-discriminations.

Indeed, at this point I want to reiterate that we (our species) are all "sinners": we *all* lack moral seriousness. As many religious commentators of various stripes, including the Buddha and John Calvin, have argued, our species flaw pervades our morality, behaviour, feelings and routine mental functioning. It is not that *some of us* may be identified as failures; we *all* share a deep moral defect. It has even been argued that our biological success and religious mission to "go forth and multiply" has led directly to untenable population levels and accompanying anthropogenic climate change. Alongside this, the huge increase in our numbers swamps each of us as an individual, so that we may indeed, as Sartre put it, feel "*de trop*", gratuitous, surplus to requirements. It may be that this very interplay of forces between memory of and suitability for (now lost) small communities, contemporary mass civilization and a pressure to achieve as individuals fuels increasing despair at the impossibility of counting or standing out in this context. Put differently, we are maddened, failed by our own overcrowding.

This defect has perverted our very language and social values. We can and we do engage in sophistry in the midst of personal immorality and global disorder. We can and we do ignore fellow human beings who suffer terribly, and we condone fellow culprits, when it suits us to do so, which is much of the time. The semantic perplexity we run into here must be closely related to a primal unwillingness or inability to be honest and straightforward. We might call it an epidemic *akrasia*. It is unfashionable and unattractive to speak in such terms but this does not render the position untenable.

If I call myself a failure it can let me off the hook. "Don't expect anything better from me, you can see what a mess I am." If I want to distract you from focusing on my moral faults, dubious actions and corrupt lifestyle, I can "scapegoat" others, subalterns, by pointing to their (sometimes more visible) failings. If I want to "big myself up" in one way or another, I can demonstrate my cleverness, beauty, athletic prowess or commercial success and downplay other, less attractive aspects of myself. Many systems of psychotherapy and management coaching rely on reframing failure as success. I do not intend to take this enquiry down a convoluted nihilistic route but to suggest that we have many ploys at our disposal for talking our way out of our collective moral failure. Often we apprehend what has gone awry via non-linguistic means: silence, emotion, genuine dialogue, bodily states. Gemma Corradi Fiumara (1990) for example, drawing from Wittgenstein among others, criticizes "the secret arrogance of logocentrism" (the predominant linguistic assertiveness of Western, and male, thought) and pleads for *listening* to be accorded greater respect.

This position chimes well with that of David Bohm (1994), whose promotion of disciplined dialogue aims to examine thought-in-action between individuals. Bohm believes that a "systemic fault" is at work in thought and language; in other words, that thought itself (not particular lines of thought), which we so much take for granted as our inevitable guide to almost all human affairs, is deeply flawed, and compounds our various problems while apparently attempting to address them objectively and constructively. Put differently, we commonly fool ourselves by failing to observe that our best-intended efforts mislead us. But our everyday language fails us too when we append labels of failure to one person or another, or one or another group, nation and so on, instead of seeking authentic understanding and real justice.

Unless one is all-wise and magnanimous, perhaps we all have our favourite nominations for failure. I like to think I am morally above the act of looking down on others but I often catch myself indulging in mental put-downs. I enjoy the secretly politically incorrect free zone of guilty pleasures inside my head, as I imagine many do, where one can undetected scoff at diverse pariahs, bums, white trash, chavs, bimbos, untouchables *et al.* (I know a teacher who openly refers scathingly to the "plebs, peasants and pond life" he encounters in the rough area of the city in which he works.) But another of my recurring targets, highly suitable for shy, non-entrepreneurial, poor underachievers, is the kind of person who is outwardly successful but easily consigned to the category of superficial, greedy, empty airhead. Almost any celebrity will do but watch the wide array of television programmes dedicated to competitive cookery, property development and entrepreneurialism for good examples. All these ambitious people chasing money and fame should know as I do that what comes out of your mouth matters more than what goes in (Jesus) and that property is theft (Proudhon); they should know, as Diogenes and Spinoza pointed out, that worldly ambition is vulgar and pointless. But they don't know these things because they are, unlike me, intellectual failures with no depth of moral insight at all! Now, given that I have some theological awareness of the holier-than-thou syndrome and some grasp of psychoanalytic principles of projection, I should have transcended such meanness of spirit and hypocrisy at my age, but yet again I have failed.

Against the view that each of us has a precious and real ego that must be boosted and protected from failure is the novelist John Fowles's argument, stemming from Heraclitus and the notions of chaos and hazard, that the *nemo* sits at the centre of our human existence and its illusions:

> The nemo is a man's sense of his own futility and ephemerality; of his relativity, his comparativeness; of his virtual nothingness ... All of us are failures; we all die ... Nobody wants to be a nobody. All our acts are partly devised to fill or mask the emptiness we feel at the core. (1965: 51)

Human beings think they survived some past wreck, are cast adrift from a golden age, and consequently they cling to symbolic rafts but in reality all is chance and eventually all is non-being; and we know but deny this.

The ultimate in being a self-perceived failure in the context of the language of non-being is suicide, self-annihilation. Another side of this is what we can provisionally call *being intentionally failed*. Being rejected, demoted and excluded are common experiences related to failure. As Sartre has suggested in his discussion of the origins of negation, some lives are dedicated to negation. The gaoler, the executioner, the assassin, and in a lesser way the police officer and the traffic warden, all these work partly to negate (some) others' being or to thwart their freedoms. In Roman gladiatorial times the organized spectacle of a fight to the death was said to be ended in the thumbs down that immediately preceded the loser's public humiliation and killing. In cases of psychopathological murder, torture and rape, the perpetrator wishes to impose on the victim an acute taste, often a terminal taste, of their own failure of autonomy, dignity, self-defence, biological continuity. The hatred that accompanies the humiliation of another may lead to their annihilation or, in the case of genocide, to mass murder intended to annihilate a whole people. Actively, aggressively negating others may be characterized by psychological torment ("I'll make you wish you'd never been born"), and by torture, dismemberment, triumphant cannibalism and disposal. Such extremes are usually associated with males, let us note.

Less extreme forms of other-annihilation include rejection and enjoyment of others' failure (*Schadenfreude*). Television talent shows necessarily entail a degree of public humiliation for contestants eliminated at an early stage, and then for the disappointed runners-up in the final stages. "I wish I'd never met you" is a common expression of the partner who has reached a terminal hatred in a failing relationship or marriage and annulment may be the legal end-point. "I wish I'd never had you" may be uttered by the exasperated or cruel mother to the child, who may carry this trace of rejection for a lifetime. "You're such a loser" rubs the other's nose in their failure. There are occasional instances of psychological sadism on the part of a mean-spirited teacher, say, who wants to see a certain pupil fail.

Suicide, murder and hatred embody extreme forms of negation, of personal annihilation. Lest we are tempted to imagine that the extreme feelings that go with these acts and intentions belong only to others, some psychological research reminds us that probably most of us sometimes entertain such fantasies and might well be capable of extreme acts given sufficient provocation. In a philosophical survey of various forms of active and passive nihilism centring around Nietzschean thought, Keith Ansell Pearson and Diane Morgan (2000) include references to and images of the skinning of a human being. We may discuss these matters according to the principles of failure of empathy and dignity, of human rights, but destructive impulses do not conveniently disappear. Somewhere deep inside lurks the beast in us all, the death instinct, the failure of "civilization". In Sartre's terms, "nothingness haunts being" (1958: 16).

The category of "being a success" should not be dismissed. Perhaps most people canvassed by researchers would sign up to belief in the importance of success and consider themselves quite successful. I shall leave defence of success to other writers, however. Here, let me bring on to the scene those characters from religious scriptures and the arts who appear to be failures and outcasts in mainstream social terms, yet who are often endorsed by the likes of Jesus as closer to genuine transcendental values. It is baffling to understand how so many right-wing fundamentalist American Christians can interpret Jesus' words in the New Testament as a prescription for or defence of capitalist affluence. As the psychoanalyst and social philosopher Erich Fromm (1979) declared, it is being rather than having that points the way to personal and social welfare and justice. Fromm condemned as an outright failure "the Great Promise of Unlimited Progress" created largely by the industrial revolution and boosted by post-Second World War economics and the mistaken "radical hedonism" that goes with it. Small wonder that William Desmond (2008) regards the original Cynics in the mould of Diogenes as so similar to later ascetics, anarchists, tramps, hoboes, beats, hippies and New Agers.

It is also ironic that in a poll of modern Indians, while Mahatma Gandhi was admired by a fair number, Bill Gates had a much higher approval rating (even before his philanthropy). Those who advocate voluntary poverty are clearly no longer cool. The loincloth is out, designer suits rule: failure is failure! We could however turn this example on its head. Gandhi has been criticized for not being the kindest of family men and his advocacy of non-violent resistance is considered a naive and dangerous policy for many other contexts (Tenembaum 2011). On the other hand, Gates's implementation of a vaccination programme against childhood diseases in Africa might potentially effect more durable, benevolent change than Gandhi's politics did. In the calculus of comparative moral success and failure it is not always clear who will turn out to be the real hero.

Back at the individual level, we can remember that becoming a failure – occasionally, somewhat or dramatically, in one or several domains of our being – may be good for us. The main character in Elia Kazan's novel and film *The Arrangement*, Evangelos Arness, is a highly successful advertising man with all the trappings of the economic good life, the rewards of the American dream. But something in him unconsciously recognizes the emptiness of his lifestyle and a car accident (or unconscious suicide attempt) leads him gradually to a complete transformation towards a much humbler but happier kind of existence. Stories of cancer in which people say "cancer was the best thing that ever happened to me" (the cyclist Lance Armstrong is a well-known example) attest to the transformational value of a failure event, sometimes referred to as post-traumatic growth. My own experiences of failed relationships, jobs and projects, however painful at the time, have probably all taught me something about life's unpredictability (and hubris) and about my (and human) resilience. One's fortunes in life can go up and down. It is unlikely to be any other way in the world of flux and chaos that governs our moral luck.

6. Learning from failure

At first sight it seems that we might want to distance ourselves from failure altogether, as if it is bad luck or tempting fate to even think about it. As the very title of Carol Tavris and Elliot Aronson's *Mistakes Were Made (But Not by Me)* (2007) makes plain, denial is a common stance. Alternatively, it is easy to fall for platitudes about "learning from our mistakes". Almost at the other end of the spectrum, when we seriously attempt to learn from catastrophes we have the call to "look the worst full in the face" (Clarke 2006: ix). The *almost* in the previous sentence points to the domain beyond learning, where failure is so terrifying or apocalyptic that some will envisage the end of the world in religious terms (the "end times") or in such dark personal terms that suicide appears the only possible response.

In one sense, perhaps the grimmest scenarios are unavoidable and cannot properly be learned from so as to effect improvement or escape. Here I mean human biological entropy, resulting in everyone's inescapable individual death, the future demise of the entire biosphere itself, of the earth and the universe. Scientists are confident that all this is inevitable: everything ultimately must fail to endure. This is, of course, denied in some quarters. Many religions insist on the reality of a life after death in some viable form. A minority of "extreme scientists" researching the causes of ageing (and rightfully monitored by critical ethicists) believe that sooner or later human death will be postponed by up to hundreds of years by new discoveries. There are, too, those scientists committed to developing the means to travel to other planets so that when the earth's resources are depleted we can continue as a species elsewhere.

The religious case for an afterlife is not disprovable, it is simply extremely implausible, but a high level of scepticism seems warranted. Scepticism, as a lifelong philosophical sceptic like Paul Kurtz (2010) conceives of it, is not a flat-out or dismissive rejection of such beliefs but contains a diversity of thoroughgoing analytical attitudes to enquiry. As for the above scientists who seek to discover life-extension technologies, we may adopt either a precautionary ethical analysis of their aims or an interested "wait and see" attitude but the hoped for outcomes of these projects, lying so far in the future, cannot be disproved as possibilities either. What we surely must keep in mind, however, is that humans have previously been incorrect about many things (the flat earth, the sun revolving around the earth); and common human imagination has often failed until a pioneer creates or discovers something previously inconceivable.

We cannot prevent our own deaths nor guarantee against the eventual dissolution of all our parts but we can improve the quality of our lives, dodge some diseases and slightly delay death by means of timely medical screening and treatment, avoidance of toxic substances and high-risk situations, good nutrition and exercise. (I am conscious that the "we" here does not apply to millions of people in the developing world.) Many failed to see the dangers of cigarette smoking and died prematurely as a consequence, for example. Here, learning from failure is very clear. Smoking involves the failure to resist short-term pleasure, the moral failure of tobacco companies and governments to be honest and to act accordingly, and perhaps the moral failure of bystanders to speak out and to act. But even in the midst of a decades-long period of learning, some smokers wish to assert their right to the civil liberty to smoke and determine their own health risks. Fair enough, perhaps, since we do not forbid boxing, hang-gliding, mountaineering, high-level alcohol consumption, anorexia nervosa and other high-risk activities, although we do hold as illegal the consumption of many drugs. I think we must conclude that we fail as a society to draw up and agree on fair and comprehensive ethical and legal attitudes to risk assessment, responsibilities and costs. We are largely confused and hypocritical, as if we do not have the collective moral will or are torn between optimal freedoms and the outlawing of risks.

Each of us may ask: does life itself meet my hopes and expectations or fail to do so? What are the failures I see around me – moral, social, economic, political – that need not continue as failures? In what ways have I failed and how do I propose to address these? Does it make sense for me to think of myself as a failure? Who do I know or who do I look up to as an example of success? Do I accept success and failure as two sides of the same coin of life? Is there some way out of failure altogether? Who can I trust to guide me?

It's possible to consider two extreme attitudes towards failure. First, one can adopt a philosophy of negation or total overcoming of failure. Here, we could turn to Christian Science and its doctrine of complete faith in Jesus Christ, which permits of no doubt and promises complete deliverance from sickness and death. Indeed, evil, error and death are regarded as illusions. While Christian Science isn't taken seriously as a rigorous philosophy, some categorize it as a form of philosophical idealism. Jarringly, Nietzschean philosophy can also be placed in this failure-transcending position in its refusal to accept the Christian and Western submission to weakness and a master–slave morality. Nietzsche's "That which does not kill me makes me stronger" has become a popular exhortation to overcome fear. Both the above views espouse a superhuman aspiration. Both are unrealistic in so far as occasional accidents and illnesses are unavoidable and often early wounds leave us weaker rather than stronger.

The alternative extreme is represented by those philosophies, philosophers and intellectuals who find life so flawed that it should be disappointedly or nihilistically written off in one way or another. Beckett, Benatar, Camus, Cioran, Houellebecq and Schopenhauer might all belong here, if with different takes on life's absurdity and painfulness. Benatar's analysis of the "self-deceptive indifference to the harm of coming into existence" (2006: 225) and his conclusions regarding the harmfulness of having further children ("the duty not to procreate") lead him to a position far too extreme for most people's tastes. Falling roughly in the same pessimistic camp, however, Joshua Foa Dienstag's book *Pessimism* (2006) includes Camus, Cioran, Miguel de Cervantes, Freud, Giacomo Leopardi, Nietzsche, Rousseau, Schopenhauer and Miguel de Unamuno, and denies that pessimism is identical with cynicism, nihilism and scepticism (or unhappiness); rather, it contains a fortitude comparable with Stoicism. Acknowledging that life (or large chunks of it) is a failure results in an array of negative views, not simply one!

The philosophers focusing on linguistic and discourse analysis have alerted us to the many ways in which language dictates, distorts and limits our experiences and perceptions. In everyday language use, something is successful or unsuccessful, a success or failure, perfect or flawed, orderly or disordered. In reality, things often sit or shift somewhere midway in a grey area, or they fluctuate from pole to pole; experiences are context-dependent. We can say that some things are mediocre rather than excellent or terrible. In some circumstances we assign numerical values to show *some* subtlety (but not much). For example, British degree classifications are given as 1st, 2:1, 2:2 or 3rd and students' essays are still often marked in spurious percentage terms as if 67 per cent is really distinguishable from 68 per cent. But language is poor at tracking and representing moving complexities, moods, paradoxes and the fine grain of human subjective existence. One can feel unaccountably free in the midst of disaster, gloomy in the midst of outward triumph, and a whole range of nameless feelings in between. A growing literature of philosophy analysing vagueness looks at just such linguistic phenomena, where non-mathematical discourse fails to be precise. In my own terms, I would call this an aspect of linguistic entropy. As time goes by and complexity increases, the original need for, and clarity of, language becomes disordered: Babelian prattle, misunderstanding, deception and mental chatter increase. Yet we can barely imagine ourselves without language – and thought – or even with a significantly pared-down language.

We might quip that the best way to deal with failure is simply to avoid it, which in some arenas we may be able to; alternatively we may embrace it. Avoid all obvious risks phobically; or, contrarily, meet risks by throwing yourself at them, counter-phobically; or, wherever possible, insure yourself against risks so that compensation always awaits you. Stories already exist of rich people who are able to insure themselves against many disasters, so that a mere phone call will produce a helicopter to whisk them and any co-insured away from a disaster scene to a five-star hotel where they can recover in luxury. The very concept of fail-safe measures means that failure is expected but damage is limited.

One "good response" to personal failure is authentic acceptance. Think of the phrase "a good loser"; this captures the sense of being a gracious failure. Instead of complaining at one's loss of hope and feeling sorry for oneself it is sometimes possible to "take it on the chin": the best man got the job or the girl. Socrates accepted his death sentence. In the very attitude of gracious acceptance the failure is lightened. The person who genuinely accepts that she or he has no special entitlement to success, who may even be pleased for the winner and who can shrug off emotional hurt, can be regarded as attractively virtuous. This is not the same as feigning acceptance or rolling over defeated, but a wise situation-specific response.

A common reaction to the topic of failure is to half-deny its existence, massage it away or reframe it positively. An example from neurolinguistic programming is to claim that there is no such thing as failure, but only "feedback". A failed business enterprise may spur one to investigate the causes of the failure, learn from them and start up another business, this time a successful one. Indeed, masses of business books are built on exactly this premise: that everything is useful information on which to build improvements. Paul Ormerod, in a highly intelligent analysis of failure recognizing the ubiquity and inevitability of failure entitled *Why Most Things Fail* (2005), concludes that, in business at least, only due action and innovation can be relied upon. Alternatively, at the personal level, you could learn that this business or any business is not the way forwards for you: you have learned that your talents lie in creative pursuits instead. This is a win–win mentality, with the glass always half full or more.

The engineering response to failure has a feeling of sound pragmatism about it:

> The causes of failures can be as many and as muddled as their lessons. When something goes wrong with a computer program or an engineering structure, the scrutiny under which the ill-fated object comes often uncovers a host of other innocuous bugs and faults that might have gone forever unnoticed had the accident not happened.   (Petroski 1992: 204)

Scrutiny is necessary and is as objective as possible in the service of discovery and prevention of future harm. But it can also lead to retrogressive discoveries of multiple, layered failure, here described as bugs and faults.

It is sobering perhaps to realize that in some domains we need failure. First, some failures are simply inevitable statistically. Second, we cannot have the kind of planet and life forms we have without some risk and error; an imaginary life with absolutely no risk and error would be neither possible nor desirable. Our psychological vigilance and our very immune system, key features for humans and other animals, help to define us. Third, failures and disappointments can teach us humility by eroding pride and hubris; and indeed we may agree with Jacques Lacan's view that in domains such as psychoanalysis errors are revealing and fertile. But fourth, evolutionary and competitive processes mean that the only way we can select the best people for certain tasks is to subject many to direct rivalry, for example special secret-service agents, astronauts, some surgeons. Those tested for toughness, decision-making and other skills by selective pressures emerge as leaders in their fields, and those who perform in a substandard way will be directed to other tasks and careers. This is often an unpalatable thought but anyone who urgently needs the help of specialists with high-level competencies will appreciate that the less good should be deselected, or failed.

Discovery-oriented failure investigations often result in useful learning, but not invariably. A medical examination may discover a cancer that is so aggressive and well developed that no practical lessons can be learned. The lesson is frankly one of doom: you are going to die, and very soon. Some may not want to know this and some will deny it or rapidly marshal religious belief to quash its emotional impact. We might say that for some this discovery is useful. Even if it is too late to modify the cancer, there may be time to put affairs in order, to make peace with oneself and others. Discovering the facts behind the thalidomide scandal in the early 1960s could do nothing to reverse the terrible deformities it caused but would help to prevent a recurrence. Police and profiler investigations into serial killers may help to detect future killers sooner.

This last point does trigger the realization of the problem of risk-elimination as depicted in Philip K. Dick's short story "The Minority Report", later made into a film. A process of Precrime utilizes "precogs" (specialized humans wired up to detect imminent crimes) as part of a futuristic scenario of crime prevention in the service of utopian aspirations. Perhaps we would all like to avoid fatal or personally damaging failures but the reality of any total banishment of failure would also have its chillingly dystopian aspects. Vigilance is an understandable and necessary human function but those who are personally hyper-vigilant usually suffer from it. Perhaps this raises the possibility that social hyper-vigilance might ironically also tip over into something dysfunctional. Nazism's "final solution" to perceived social and ethnic problems is one of the most glaring illustrations of this point. The longing for prelapsarian utopias tends to create dangerous fantasies of the metalapsarian utopia or heavenly city that is finally beyond all failure and disappointment.

A more down-to-earth response to failure awareness, common in education, the professions and business, is to call for continuous improvement in practice and training. Realistic about the occurrence of failure, especially human error, this approach commends, even insists upon, constant updating of knowledge and skills so as to give the best possible chance of avoiding or minimizing, for example, falling behind in education, losing one's edge and falling foul of malpractice traps in the professions and staying competitive in product development and sales in business. Now, this very common position seems to sit midway between pragmatism and idealism. On the one hand, hospitals and businesses recognize that identifying and learning from failure is crucial to avoiding disasters and setbacks, therefore non-defensive openness is an important strategy. On the other hand, the cult of excellence and machismo pervading many organizations can work against admissions of weakness and failure. Amy C. Edmondson argues that a new paradigm is needed "that recognizes the inevitability of failure in today's complex work environment in which mistakes multiply" (2011: 55). This approach stands a good chance of succeeding provided that it doesn't succumb to empty reification, that is, "Let's openly learn from failure, admit our mistakes and constantly improve ourselves" should not unwittingly turn into a vacuous mantra.

One of the ways in which we have always learnt from our design errors and limitations is to improve on ourselves with technology.

Toolmaking from earliest times has enabled us to hunt, defend ourselves, store food, transport materials and construct dwellings. The Industrial Revolution exponentially accelerated technology and the information revolution has gone much further still. Computers rapidly, routinely and accurately perform tasks that we perform inefficiently. A large part of this macro-trend in human progress consists of health and medical technological improvement, one part of which is prosthetics, or artificial anatomical aids. Cutting-edge inventions for human enhancement include cyborgs, nano-machines and robots that may augment, repair and replace humans in various ways. Where we contain or *are* biological kluges, our own conscious designs can greatly reduce or eliminate many of our own flaws. To what extent such developments turn out to be desirable, failure-proof and non-dystopian remains to be seen but the transcendence of human failure is clearly a major goal.

The topic of perfectibility (or corrigibility) sits uncomfortably alongside the tacit question of what lives are worth. Moral philosopher John Broome, in his *Weighing Lives* (2004), compares the qualities of individual lives in terms of their well-being, supportive medical costs and matters of population control. He admits that such questions become very uncomfortable and they certainly challenge egalitarian human-rights assumptions, at least hypothetically: are some lives worth more than others, or are some more painful and costlier to maintain than others, and what are we to think about these questions as individuals, citizens and policy-makers? That some of us contain or embody more physical or mental "failings" than others is hard to dispute, yet for obvious reasons open discussion of such issues borders on taboo. However, research progress in genetics and applications in genetic engineering and genetic counselling already force us to confront such matters. In some parts of the world male lives are esteemed more highly than females lives, and practices of gender-selective abortion and (female) infant abandonment are not uncommon.

Readers hardwired for optimism or freely choosing it will have despaired at the extent to which I have neglected success while presenting failure as ubiquitous. A popular business writer such as Steve McDermott, whose *How to be a Complete and Utter Failure in Life, Work and Everything* (2007) is built on faith in his own humour, self-promotional savvy, banalities and scathing paradox, is unlikely to be impressed. In so far as success and failure have real meaning, of course, they must share the stage or alternate in some way. It seems only fair that we acknowledge the upside and transcendence of failure. In a sense, all narratives of light conquering darkness speak of this transcendence: that there is something rather than nothing, the winter solstice, the phoenix rising from the ashes, Jesus rising from the dead, good triumphing over evil, hope over despair, human ingenuity and technology over many obstacles. These contain a mixture of myths of defiance and realities. Successful pop stars such as Madonna are said to have constantly reinvented themselves, successful businesses remain innovative, and successful marriage partners work hard at communication and stay on their toes.

We are told "If it ain't broke, don't fix it" but we can retort that if at first a thing appears not to be broken, just look much more closely: the micro-cracks are always there. Indeed, university students are traditionally encouraged not to take anything at face value but to critique and problematize. Mark Twain wrote in a letter in 1887, "All you need in this life is ignorance and confidence, and then success is sure". Failure is often more honest than success, more true to authentic humanness. You may work very hard without it leading to wealth or success. Material success often requires calculating competitiveness, self-distortion, lies and disregard for others. "Failures" often concede that they cannot keep up the pretences required for success. Many philosophers (e.g. Cioran, Nietzsche, Sartre) in fact have specifically sought contexts decoupled from academic institutions so that they might think and write freely. Diogenes today would fail to secure an academic philosophy post, even in the specialism of Cynicism, even if he wanted it! "Successes" may buy themselves better health care and live a little longer but they must also succumb to biological failure. Bigshots and nobodies alike have relatively brief ontic and worldly status before eternal forgottenness and non-being.

In the longest-term picture of entropic run-down, there is no final redemption: once extinguished, the universe is not going to reassemble itself, God cannot pull anything out of the hat (especially since he himself/it itself is now a depleted symbol). Long term, even though we will not be around to witness, document or lament it, the universe will fail, the earth having failed and the sun died long before that ultimate event. For some philosophers such as Jean-François Lyotard, factoring inevitable ultimate solar catastrophe into our thinking presents a "transcendental trauma for philosophy" (Brassier 2003). But somehow we have to hold in mind simultaneously both the personal and social irrelevance for us of solar death some billions of years away and its meaning for us as a forward-looking species. Just as our own deaths usually remain at the back of our minds while we conduct relatively carefree, somewhat successful lives, so it would be ridiculous for solar death to preoccupy us. However, as science produces more success strategies it also suggests probabilistic limitations. We may extend the human lifespan, conquer many diseases and travel further into space, but we will still die, new diseases and challenges will arise, and distant space travel and extraterrestrial settlement seems permanently unlikely.

One outstanding phenomenon introduces uncertainty into this scenario. Gottfried Leibniz's question about why there is something rather than nothing continues to nag at philosophy and physics. We can ask where creativity in general comes from, for example in Shakespeare, The Beatles' music, literature, science, technology and record-breaking sports achievements. Where do great new thinkers and activists "come from"? We can of course make the claim that any team of chimpanzees with the right equipment and sufficient time can match all such achievements but this remains counter-intuitive. It is difficult to refute the notion that behind every significant renewal (rebirth, novelty, *creatio ex nihilo*, resurrection, invention, discovery, revolution, negentropy) lies some indisputable counter-entropic force. The German term *Trotzmacht des Geistes* conveys this sense of a vital spirit that opposes negative forces. This phenomenon is not always heroic in character, nor is it always the product of hard work; it may be random, playful and spontaneous. Its big problem, then, is that it cannot necessarily be commanded or made formulaic. Sad to say, while this momentarily counter-entropic triumphant force has perennial characteristics, it is also subject to macro-entropy. Authentic early Christianity succumbed to Roman and subsequent bastardization. The Roman Empire itself perished. The Beatles split up. Democracy has lost a great deal of its meaning. And so on. This cyclical pattern of birth, death and rebirth may be translated into the terminology of successful creation, the prospect of failure and transcendence of failure.

The inevitability of large-scale collapses need not be greeted with despair. Thomas Homer-Dixon, for example, in *The Upside of Down* (2006), discusses the concept of "catagenesis" or "renewal through breakdown": a kind of phoenix-rising-from-the-ashes view. This is not a Pollyannaish minimization of disaster but a recommendation to learn from failure and prepare creatively for new tactics. Similarly to what I have said about entropy, underlying fallibility, faultlines, cracks and major failures, Homer-Dixon suggests that foreshocks (whether regarding the stock market or earthquakes) warn us of impending peril. At a personal level, health scares and marital arguments can alert us to worse trouble brewing; at a global level, rising temperatures, melting glaciers and extreme weather events may warn us that far worse is in store. In both cases, we contributed to the escalating problems but failed to notice or take due responsibility; in both cases we still have the choice to own up and act responsibly, or bury our head in the sand. And in both cases, whatever we do, the worst may materialize and may be temporarily terrible and unsettling. But both could lead to renewal: new relationships or self-discoveries; a new civilization based on new values and technologies. Portents, augurs, omens have existed from antiquity, and they remain highly fallible.

To my knowledge there is no study of failure as such, no attempt to quantify failure across domains, philosophical studies like those by Ricoeur (1986) and Roberts (2011) notwithstanding. Anecdotally we are well aware that many businesses fail, weather forecasts fail, relationships break down, hopefully composed poetry and novels never see the light of day, and so on. Probably, however, for many of us failure seems an occasional event only: the odd misfortune or even disaster in the domains of relationships, jobs, health. Only occasionally do we get that terrible phone call, see that truck hurtling towards us, hear the bank manager denying us further credit. Many inhabitants of sunny Southern California enjoy such good living conditions that they can ignore the ever-present threat but rare occurrence of deadly earthquakes. Everyday life for many of us probably seems to run fairly smoothly in an uneventful pattern most of the time, except, that is, for what we may call minor hiccups and irritations: your alarm doesn't wake you up; there's no cereal; your child is ill; the car won't start; there's a traffic jam; you can't seem to find a parking space.

We all learn in a trial-and-error fashion to respond to these challenges appropriately. Some are faced "philosophically": it won't kill you to miss breakfast or be late for work once in a while. Now move up a level, where these things happen far too often. Here, you might reckon that your urban existence is too stressful and consider moving to the country and finding an easier job; that is, you face this situation by taking practical remedial actions. Now move to another level, where the novelty of your remedial action has worn off and new irritations arise: you have fewer friendship-support networks, less money and so on. You might, at another level, turning towards political philosophy, start to question the very nature of twenty-first-century, capitalist treadmill, alienated existence; you could join an anarchist commune; or invite Jesus into your heart. You might despair, or consider suicide; you might become depressed or get ill (and remember that in very different ways the existentialist philosopher and the psychoanalyst might interpret your depression or illness as bad faith or defence mechanisms).

Somehow most of us get through irritating moments, bad days and sticky patches in our lives, especially when there is an underlying resilience. But if you were unlucky enough to have had previous difficult times (being abandoned as a child, death of a parent, serious illness, say) those may have helped you cope with present adversity *or* they may have weakened your resolve and problem-solving capacities. And if you are very unlucky you might get more than your share of adversity. Let's say you are struggling with your new lifestyle in the country, then out of the blue you get a cancer diagnosis or you lose your job, or both. Many people would crack under these circumstances, some might seek counselling or psychotherapy, and a few might kill themselves. Personality, personal history, present circumstances and available support will all combine to lead to defeat, triumph or a "successful" muddling through.

It's probably wise to pause to remember how absurd all this can sound to the average ear. In Woody Allen's film *Whatever Works* (2009), the lead character Boris Yellnikoff is the quintessential curmudgeon. Always sounding off about everything from chaos and entropy to our miserable "failed species" and the "inchworms" he is surrounded by, Boris is clever and amusing but eventually tedious. The upshot of the film, which shows him surviving an aborted academic career, ongoing neuroses, suicide attempts and failed marriages, is that he "totally lucks out" in finding a new love and speaks with redemptive affection of the wisdom of giving and taking whatever love one can in this uncertain existence.

We can and we should remind ourselves that failure as a phenomenon can be exaggerated and furthermore that predictions about future failures and catastrophes have frequently been wrong. There appears to be a common human craving for certainty that, combined with mechanisms of bias, can override reality. Predictions about the end of the world have a very long lineage, some of them from religious quarters being embarrassingly specific and by definition always incorrect. Dan Gardner's *Future Babble* (2011) has copious examples of predictions made by experts and their embarrassing failure to come to pass. However, we must always evaluate significant new predictions on their own merits. For example, as individuals and governments we have to decide quite urgently whether climate change is real and anthropogenic, and what to do about it. If real and as serious as many claim, then failure to take due action may result in decimation of the world's population within decades. If the evidence is inaccurate or the picture more complex than we currently know, it may turn out that we have been deceived and wasted anxiety and money on strategies for combating it. The big problem is that our science is a long way from being capable of the kinds of accurate predictions we need. What a science of failure might do is to (i) insist on identifying discrete domains of failure and suitable methods of quantification, and (ii) probe for the existence of any reliable cross-domain characteristics. But to my knowledge this kind of science does not exist.

While certain industries and institutions do focus on failure for good reasons, one can see little appetite for developing the kind of convergent, cross-disciplinary study implied by Joel Fisher's (2010) "anaprokopology". To some extent Joseph T. Hallinan's (2009) "errornomics" and Kathryn Schulz's (2010) "wrongology" are also stabs in this same dark direction. Those involved in risk assessment, health-and-safety audits, catastrophe studies, Holocaust and other studies all have excellent reasons for establishing a knowledge base that might ensure certain moral atrocities don't happen again, or are anticipated or mitigated. The idea that links exist across all failure phenomena isn't usually entertained. I suppose we might argue that different failure-like phenomena – from, say, various domains and magnitudes – cannot be legitimately lumped together. How are earthquakes, wars, car accidents, disease processes, botched surgery, business failures, fallacious arguments and broken marriages, and death itself, meaningfully linked? Some, for example, are clearly beyond human control. But many are not. And all demand human responses. All are studied. Many are brought about or exacerbated by faulty judgements, corner cutting and cognitive errors. In fact, even the worst natural disasters are studied and prepared for, in urgent practical terms but also as a matter of psychological interest: different personalities respond somewhat differently to the same disasters. What do philosophies of stoicism, pragmatism, pessimism and idealism have to say about differential responses? We are quite keen to promote problem solving in education but far less genuinely enthusiastic about radical problematizing: that is, identifying and exploring how things break down.

But to take a counter attitude to this, we can quite reasonably argue that at a personal level failures need not be anticipated or learned from. It is stressful and unnecessary to constantly prepare for failure. Given the *relative* rarity of major failures in our lives, perhaps it is wisest to live at least close to the present, to eat, drink and be merry, and to meet failure and its emotional and other kinds of fallout only when actually necessary. For example, rather than worrying chronically about the possibility of bad things happening, react to them when they do occur with all the short-term grief, cursing and emergency behaviours we have at our disposal. Crying, many would say, is a natural and perhaps necessary response to bad news, perhaps sometimes healthier than convoluted intellectual strategies for attempted sidestepping of psychological suffering.

In reality, in line with the homely advice to "try, try again" when we don't at first succeed, we may remember that most learning involves repeated initial failures. Our early attempts to learn to crawl, walk and speak are always accompanied by falls and errors. It is quite rare that anyone's very first girlfriend or boyfriend turns out to be their lifelong partner or that the first job you walk into is the one you happily stay with. Very few people excel at golf, ice skating or tightrope walking at their first try. As Lewis Thomas put it, writing about general biological themes: "We learn, as we say, by 'trial and error.' Why do we always say that? Why not 'trial and rightness' or 'trial and triumph'? The old phrase puts it that way because that is, in real life, the way it is done" (1988: 170).

The world of counselling and psychotherapy (and also stress management, resilience building, happiness creation and coaching) is made up of analyses of, and remedies for, personal failures, whether these be the effects of parental inadequacy, traumatic life events, learned helplessness, faulty personal logic, bad luck, addictive behaviours or whatever. Unfortunately this is a bewildering world of multiple theories and competing clinical professions, which even in its own terms fails perhaps 20 per cent of its clients. But it can be supported by the kind of philosophy of listening advocated by Corradi Fiumara (1990) and by the practice of receptivity found in Zen Buddhism and elsewhere. The talking therapies, whatever their own flaws (which are many), hold out the offer of deep interpersonal dialogue and emotion-honouring that is not always available in books, self-help and what we might call macho-stoical solipsism. One may courageously find fortitude within oneself but the strong social element of our evolutionary make-up means that often solutions or support are found in our fellow humans, however fallible and sometimes disappointing they turn out to be.

One thing we learn from a scan of psychotherapeutic theories is that they have conflicting epistemologies as regards the nature of being human, of suffering, and recovery. Broadly speaking, the psychoanalytic approaches recognize a somewhat faulty psychic structure full of unconscious conflicts and defence mechanisms, the effects of which can be partially ameliorated through therapy. Some forms of psychoanalysis take death, entropy and brute suffering seriously in the concept of the death drive. The psychoanalyst Rob Weatherill, for example, drawing on Lacan and Jean Baudrillard, complains that "the profession has been hugely oversold in a world-wide evangelism of human potential, which has taken flight from any notion of the brute real" (1998: 143). The texts supporting the humanistic therapies (many of these emanating from California) tend to have a somewhat, sometimes relentless, upbeat flavour, encouraging clients to think of themselves as unimpeded self-actualizers. Cognitive behavioural therapies, again by contrast, focus on individuals' cognitive errors and related behavioural limitations, and seek to re-educate clients. What most of these lack in their conceptual foundations is much, if any, reference to relevant philosophy, sociology and biology. In this sense they can be considered incomplete or flawed epistemologies.

One school of psychotherapy that is based directly on philosophical insights (like Ellis's rational emotive behaviour therapy, which draws from Stoicism) is existential therapy, which makes therapeutic inferences from Sartre and Heidegger in particular. For some, authenticity is the cornerstone of this approach:

> Authenticity can provide an ethical grounding that can underlie all our other values. If values are chosen in an authentic way then there is a sense that one can succeed or fail in being true to one's self. That is, we can act or fail to act in accordance with the values we have authentically chosen.
>
> (Pollard 2005: 174)

Two of existential therapy's planks are authenticity and courage. Faced with cancer one might be heroic about it, yet such courageous behaviour might not be fully authentic. If genuine, one might simply be terrified, feel a lot of pain, and die an undignified death. Lisa Diedrich examines exactly such experiences of cancer and of the "failure of the body, of conventional and alternative medicine, and of language" (2005: 135). There are times when fragility trumps courage, indeed when the flesh is so weak as to let down the spirit completely. *The courage to be* is a nice, deep, motivational slogan, with heavy-duty theological and philosophical wheels on it, but sometimes you just want to pull the duvet over your fragile head and make the world go away. It is questionable whether existential therapy is any more successful than other psychotherapies.

Touted as a breakthrough in understanding "the secret fear of failure", Petruska Clarkson's *The Achilles Syndrome* (1994) examined the "secret flaw" of many outwardly successful people. Her book contains examples of the "pseudocompetency" or shameful, phoney excellence experienced and often concealed by high achievers and how this can be overcome. She included references to stressed doctors and psychotherapists in this book, mentioning their high suicide rate. Yet in 2006, Clarkson – a distinguished and multi-qualified therapist, referred to by some close colleagues as a "deeply tortured soul" – killed herself by overdose. Of course there are debates to be had about whether suicide constitutes failure, whether it nullifies what someone has achieved, and so on. But we must surely always ask what the grounds are for confidence in any enterprise like psychotherapy, philosophy, religion, commerce or politics where public claims are made along the lines of "follow this prescription and durable success will surely follow". Many of us appear susceptible to such exaggerated claims.

Sometimes, in life and therapy, we apparently learn nothing. *This* time my (hairdressing, floristry, restaurant, massage) business will succeed; *this* is surely the right man for me; *this* time I'm staying off the booze for good. We may have a kind of foolhardy courage and resolution without concomitant wisdom and humility: failure returns and returns. *We* have constructed the most successful form of psychotherapy; *ours* is more rational and sophisticated than others. In the same way we are bound to think today that one school of philosophy is superior to others and certainly superior to the various philosophical schools of the ancient Greeks. Yet all are part of the same error-spotting, fault-overcoming reasoning process, and all are highly fallible.

Another take on failure is that, like all other generalized phenomena, regardless of what I or anyone else thinks about it, the world does what it does independently and indifferently, and each of us construes it according to our personality biases. In other words, the assumption of universal rationality fails, it must defer to the principle of individual phenomenology. The success-oriented, who probably also believe in omnipresent hope and happiness, will see success and its prospects everywhere, just as the religious will always see God in everything. Those who are failure-oriented, who *may* have depressive personalities, will see failure everywhere. Those with personalities set on moderation will always see both sides of an argument! And those like the existentialist group therapist Irvin Yalom promote therapeutic hope, fellow solidarity, the ventilation of emotion and the overcoming of Schopenhauerian despair. In his novel *The Schopenhauer Cure*, Yalom understands Schopenhauer better than he understood himself in a way that is similar to my observation about Kierkegaard in the previous chapter of this book.

I have elsewhere in this book despaired of religion and also one of its common prescriptions, living in the present moment. The Christian concept of providence and Buddhist mindfulness coincide in a kind of recipe for post-lapsarian living. Regrets, guilt and depression about past failures and the flawed nature of existence, together with anxieties about the likelihood of future failures, can be located in the human mind. The mind itself, or that vast part of it that is demonstrably dysfunctional, is a kluge, a crooked instrument that operates iteratively on the basis of hit-or-miss efforts to match reality against its inner-linguistic maps, always adapting reluctantly, clunking on with its fallible hardware and software: thought itself resists self-correction. That thought itself is flawed, contains a systemic flaw, and distorts all that it touches is a proposition put forward by Bohm (1994) and explored a great deal by the mystic philosopher Krishnamurti, who collaborated in many dialogues with Bohm. If the kind of individual, authentic, embodied "mystical" experience of enlightenment and nirvana associated with the Buddha and others were less elusive and many more of us could live skilfully with moment-to-moment-specific cognitive fluidity, there might be much more hope of humanity exiting its pained, flawed human condition.

If it is accepted that decay and death "haunt" us, permeate our existence even as we try alternately to deny and confront them, then there is some chance that the lives we make for ourselves will be somewhat courageous and authentic in the existentialist tradition. Heidegger's "being-towards-the-end" challenges us all. Death is the ultimate failure of the organism and is indeed evident all around us (or was until we in the West hid it so well). I have argued that failure in its myriad forms permeates human life and all natural phenomena. How this realization impacts on each person may depend on temperament. Personally, I find it somehow comforting to know roughly where I stand and where I end, and knowledge of my own failings brings me to self-acceptance rather than to melancholy. Of course, such knowledge isn't a conveniently packaged matter occurring only once but something recurring to us throughout life, presuming that we do not take the suicide option that is sometimes a temptation.

I like to think that the bottom line in learning from failure is that, along with success, it has no real substance. The success–failure polarity is in an important sense imaginary or exaggerated (except in some occupations, such as nuclear power safety and surgery!). Yes, you lost that tennis match, you didn't pass your driving test, you haven't written the great twenty-first-century novel or attracted interest in your invention. Or, yes, you made your first million at the age of twenty-five, you married the person you set your heart on, you launched that humanitarian campaign that saves lives, your IVF treatment worked. It is claimed that a Japanese temple-building company, Kongō Gumi, was in business for 1,400 years and then failed. But so what? If one thing didn't work or fail, or failed after a long period of success, something else would always happen.

Whatever is going on in your life, you can only eat and drink so much, the sun shines and the rain falls equally on everyone, accidents can befall anyone. It is tempting to make the familiar case that the "failures" are closer to heaven, or to counter-assert that the successful tend to attract yet more success. But we are all born and we all die. Most of us have our ups and downs, the vicissitudes of little successes and failures punctuating each other across the life course. Perhaps almost any of us is eligible to win the lottery of at least a few moments of grace, a little bliss that is related neither to failure nor to success but simply to being alive.

Postscript

I have presented an argument in this book for a grand scheme of failure. Grand narratives are a little out of fashion these days, as is negativity generally. If you want to be rich and successful, write a book on success, on happiness, self-esteem and positive psychology, on how to make money, or about guardian angels. I've lost count of how many acquaintances, when I told them I was writing this book, either pulled a disapproving face or made what they thought was a highly original joke about "Wouldn't it be funny if your book about failure became successful?" Ha ha, yes, wouldn't it? We should all be aware that yesterday's big new ideas and snappy jargon constitute today's forgotten books, sitting forlornly and anachronistically on the shelves of charity shops.

In my grand ("grandiose" if you want to put the boot in, to fail me) scheme, the universe is at best a chaos of intertwined or alternating forces of success and failure, of viability and fallibility, vitality and morbidity. Human life is always ambiguous. Being is indeed "haunted by non-being" in Sartrean terms. We should probably learn not to be surprised by failure or necessarily to take it too personally. Failure is pervasive, from original and continuing entropy, through geological and climatological phenomena, through all animal life including our own, and throughout all human epistemologies, inventions, institutions and relationships. Exactly how failure is distributed is unknown, probably unknowable, but chance and chaos vie with justice and order, randomness with rationality.

In our own lives, any of us may be affected to one degree or another by natural disasters and man-made catastrophes. Any of us in the wrong place at the wrong time is susceptible to the impact of randomly collapsing bridges, faulty aeroplane engines and badly driven cars. (The odds against such events are mercifully small, except for the victims.) Each of us carries a set of psychological tendencies, a casino-like biology, and experiences supportive or non-supportive social networks that will help determine our happiness or otherwise, our good and bad luck, and our eventual death. Misfortunes can strike from outside and from within. Each of us perhaps knows more or less the faults and failings we carry with us and inflict on others. At particular times through life we may become aware of near misses, warning signs, cracks in our career. Problems will be mitigated by reason and will, by friends and others.

The art of living with failure is, perhaps, built from self-knowledge, mindfulness, humour, resilience and reflection on the guidance offered by Buddhism and Stoicism. Even an atheist can derive some moral direction from Jesus; even someone weary of being called a cynic can derive inspiration from the original Cynics of antiquity. However pessimistic, one can remain open to the personalities and arguments of one's optimistic fellow human beings. Life is messy and we each take up the kluges that seem to serve us best.

By way of final personal example and to encourage readers' similar self-reckoning, my own failure calculus is roughly as follows. Entropy-wise, of course, as someone in his sixties I am not at my biological best; I cannot escape the effects of lifelong wear and tear on the body and its invisible inner lottery of failings. The basic fault bequeathed by my mother has left a modest (by some comparisons) trail of broken relationships and disappointments behind me. I may never know what sum of failings my own parenting leaves behind me long term in my sons' lives, nor can I readily disentangle my parenting errors from parenting behaviour that was beyond my noticing or correcting. My pathologically butterfly mind has created a trail of things half done, uncompleted, failed projects, if you will. One of these, for example, is an unwritten book entitled *The Imperfect Integrity of the Faint-Hearted Nihilist.*

My flaws are many: some have been modified by the years and by experience and insight, and some have probably increased. I haven't had unqualified success in my efforts to diet, exercise or change other bad habits involving money management and domestic order. Several of my household appliances and items (CD-player, gas fire, printer, complicated lightbulb fittings, etc.) still await repairs for months, even years. The boiler has just packed in, the house is cold and my small financial cushion against such events is just getting smaller. Diogenes didn't need all these comforts and luxuries but we seem to. Although my childhood shyness receded with the years and practice, occasionally even now in a social situation I will still suddenly dry up and shrink anxiously into myself, shyness operating like the break-out of a mostly dormant geological fault. I don't think I have been an outstanding moral success, in so far as I have not led a life of self-sacrifice, huge altruism or political action: I have failed to speak and act courageously. Like millions of my peers I have been a bystander as runaway capitalism and a culture of consumerism and technical-rationality with a shrinking respect for feelings, or empathic failure, has left billions poor and climate change perhaps verging on the catastrophic.

The logic of my own belief in an original-sin-like anthropathology or fallenness means that like almost all my fellow human beings I shall have lived and died with a false or "fallen" consciousness or what Slavoj Žižek refers to as cynical reason. In Buddhist terms I have remained in samsara and not known nirvana. Occasionally I imagine the true self I have failed to be, my authentic alter ego; where I am cowed by lifelong habits and fearfulness, he is free, inno-cent, fearless. Actually, he doesn't agonize over the moral problems of the world, he just doesn't dwell in or add to them; he is "without sin". But perhaps even that thought is no more than a shard of the cultural religious conditioning I cannot have altogether escaped.

It is an irresistible fantasy to imagine what a spokesperson might say at my (or your) funeral as to the balance of my (or your) success and failure. I hope I have been kind enough and that I have passed on some modest positive moral values to my children. I hope I may at last have found and given real and durable love in my closest relationship. I hope that however mistaken I may be in my analysis in these pages, I have not thereby caused any actual wilful harm. Perhaps I should hope that I am proved wrong in my negative reckoning by the social, environmental and global outcomes of the years ahead.

Further reading

While few texts can be found directly on the philosophy of failure, when failure is interpreted more broadly as sin, evil, error, inauthenticity, catastrophe and so on, much wider resources become evident. For its relative rarity and philosophical weight, Paul Ricoeur's *Fallible Man* (1986) ranks very highly. For an original and contemporary philosophical look at the theory of error across the domains of science, psychoanalysis, history and politics, and art, which also suggests significant distinctions between error and failure, John Roberts's *The Necessity of Errors* (2011) is essential reading. Alan Jacobs's *Original Sin* (2008) provides a very good overview of human moral corruption. While it is clearly not *my* "thing", anyone wanting a thorough theological exposition of original sin and its forgiveness will benefit from reading James Alison's *The Joy of Being Wrong* (1998). For those with an appetite for the idea that life itself is an irredeemable failure and disappointment, philosophers such as Schopenhauer ([1851] 1970) and aphorists such as Cioran (1998) are musts. A text making interesting links between philosophy and psychotherapy relevant to self-esteem, in self-help form, is Albert Ellis's *The Myth of Self-Esteem* (2005). Neel Burton combines psychiatric and philosophical insights into the standard distorted image of success in his *The Art of Failure* (2010).

Scott Sandage's *Born Losers* (2005) is an excellent historical account of the development of the idea of personal failure in the USA. Readers interested in a thoughtful analysis of business failure will gain much from Paul Ormerod's *Why Most Things Fail* (2005), as well as from a special edition of the *Harvard Business Review* (April 2011). Max Bazerman and Ann Tenbrunsel's *Blind Spots* (2011) is an interesting study of business ethics incorporating references to common individual cognitive errors, unethical business practice and faulty politics. Henry Petroski provides insights into engineering failures in *To Engineer is Human* (1992). Those with an interest in failure reflected through art will welcome Lisa Le Feuvre's fascinating book *Failure* (2010). Douglas Murphy's *The Architecture of Failure* (2012) looks at and into selected architectural failures past and present. In an expanding literature on critical thinking, cognitive errors and human misjudgements, Kathryn Schulz's *Being Wrong* (2010) stands out, and similarly (although with the added interest of an evolutionary and psychological take) Gary Marcus's *Kluge* (2008) offers explanations for the ubiquity of errors. I am bound to suggest my own *What's Wrong With Us?* (2007) as a hypothesis for universal human pathology. For those wanting a more light-hearted look at failure, I can recommend Stephen Pile's *The Ultimate Book of Heroic Failures* (2011). Readers will also find within the text of the present book many references to failure in relation to specific domains, such as US foreign policy, UK education, religion, politics, relationships, psychiatry and so on.

While, as I have said, there is no interdisciplinary academic study of failure as such, perhaps the nearest we get is the study of risk, and here I can recommend Baruch Fischhoff and John Kadvany's *Risk* (2011) for its concise examination of a wide array of risks, and of judgement and decision-making.

Given the sometimes contentious nature of a subject like failure, it is well worth reading a scholarly account such as Drexel Woodson's "'Failed' States, Societal 'Collapse', and Ecological 'Disaster'" (2010), which critiques grand theories of societal failure, including Jared Diamond's catastrophe theory.

References

Alejandro 2007. "I'm a Failure and I Want to Commit Suicide". Experience Project
    website.   www.experienceproject.com/stories/Think-About-Suicide/117704
    (accessed April 2012).
Alison, J. 1998. *The Joy of Being Wrong: Original Sin Through Easter Eyes*. New
    York: Crossroad.
Ansell Pearson, K. & D. Morgan (eds) 2000. *Nihilism Now! Monsters of Energy*.
    Basingstoke: Palgrave Macmillan.
Auster, P. 1998. *Hand to Mouth: A Chronicle of Early Failure*. London: Faber.
Barrett, W. 1961. *Irrational Man: A Study in Existential Philosophy*. London:
    Heinemann.
Bazerman, M. H. & A. E. Tenbrunsel 2011. *Blind Spots: Why We Fail to Do What's
    Right and What to Do About It*. Princeton, NJ: Princeton University Press.
Benatar, D. 2006. *Better Never to Have Been: The Harm of Coming Into Existence*.
    Oxford: Oxford University Press.
Bentall, R. 2010. *Doctoring the Mind: Why Psychiatric Treatments Fail*. London:
    Penguin.
Berger, J. 1965. *The Success and Failure of Picasso*. Harmondsworth: Penguin.
Bohm, D. 1994. *Thought as a System*. London: Routlege.
Bourdieu, P. 1999. *The Weight of the World: Social Suffering in Contemporary
    Society*. Cambridge: Polity.
Bourne, C. 2006. *A Future for Presentism*. Oxford: Clarendon Press.
Brassier, R. 2003. "Solar Catastrophe: Lyotard, Freud, and the Death-Drive".
    Philosophy Today 47(4): 421–30.
Broome, J. 2004. *Weighing Lives*. Oxford: Oxford University Press.
Broussard, M. (ed.) 2003. *The Dictionary of Failed Relationships*. New York: Three
    Rivers.
Bukowski, C. 1986. *You Get So Alone at Times that it Just Makes Sense*. Santa Rosa,
    CA: Black Sparrow Press.
Burton, N. 2010. *The Art of Failure: The Anti Self-Help Guide*. Oxford: Acheron.
Calder, J. 2001. *The Philosophy of Samuel Beckett*. London: Calder.
Calman, S. 2006. *Confessions of a Failed Grown-Up*. London: Pan.
Camus, A. [1942] 1975. *The Myth of Sisyphus*. London: Penguin.
Carey, J. 2005. *What Good are the Arts?* London: Faber.
Chomsky, N. 2007. *Failed States*. London: Penguin.
Cicchetti, D. & E. Walker (eds) 2003. *Neurodevelopmental Mechanisms in
    Psychopathology.* Cambridge: Cambridge University Press.
Cioran, E. M. 1998. *The Trouble with Being Born*. New York: Arcade.

Clarke, L. 2006. *Worst Cases: Terror and Catastrophe in the Popular Imagination.* Chicago, IL: University of Chicago Press.

Clarkson, P. 1996. *The Achilles Syndrome: Overcoming the Secret Fear of Failure.* Shaftesbury: Element.

Corradi Fiumara, G. 1990. *The Other Side of Language: A Philosophy of Listening.* London: Routledge.

Critchley, S. 1997. *Very Little ... Almost Nothing: Death, Philosophy, Literature.* London: Routledge.

Critchley, S. 2008. *Infinitely Demanding: Ethics of Commitment, Politics of Resistance.* London: Verso.

de Botton, A. 2004. *Status Anxiety.* London: Hamish Hamilton.

Desmond, W. 1988. "Philosophy and Failure". *Journal of Speculative Philosophy,* **2**(4).

Desmond, W. 2008. *Cynics.* Stocksfield: Acumen.

Diamond, J. 2005. *Collapse: How Societies Choose to Fail or Survive.* London: Allen Lane.

Diedrich, L. 2005. "A Bioethics of Failure: Antiheroic Cancer Narratives." In *Ethics of the Body: Postconventional Challenges*, M. Shildrick and R. Mykitiuk (eds), 135–52. Cambridge, MA: MIT Press.

Dienstag, J. 2006. *Pessimism: Philosophy, Ethic, Spirit.* Princeton, NJ: Princeton University Press.

Drees, W. B. (ed.) 2003. *Is Nature Ever Evil? Religion, Science and Value.* London: Routledge.

Dunn, J. 2000. *The Cunning of Unreason: Making Sense of Politics.* London: HarperCollins.

Edmondson, A. C. 2011. "Strategies for Learning from Failure". *Harvard Business Review* (April): 49–55.

Eliot, T. S. [1936] 2001. "Burnt Norton". In *Four Quartets.* London: Faber.

Eliot, T. S. [1922] 2002. *The Waste Land and Other Poems.* London: Faber.

Ellis, A. 2005. *The Myth of Self-Esteem.* New York: Prometheus.

Evans, G. 2006. *Educational Failure and Working Class White Children in Britain.* Basingstoke: Palgrave Macmillan.

Farmer, P. 2005. *Pathologies of Power: Health, Human Rights, and the New War on the Poor.* Berkeley, CA: University of California Press.

Feltham, C. 2007. *What's Wrong With Us? The Anthropathology Thesis.* Chichester: Wiley.

Fischhoff, B. & J. Kadvany 2011. *Risk: A Very Short Introduction.* Oxford: Oxford University Press.

Fisher, J. 2010. "Judgement and Purpose". In *Failure*, L. Le Feuvre (ed.), 116–21. London: Whitechapel Gallery.

Fowles, J. 1965. *The Aristos.* London: Pan.

Fromm, E. 1979. *To Have or To Be?* London: Abacus.

Gardiner, S. M. 2011. *A Perfect Moral Storm: The Ethical Tragedy of Climate Change.* New York: Oxford University Press.

Gardner, D. 2011. *Future Babble: Why Expert Predictions Fail and Why We Believe Them Anyway.* London: Virgin.

Graham, G. 2010. *The Disordered Mind: An Introduction to Philosophy of Mind and Mental Illness.* London: Routledge.

Gray, J. 2002. *Straw Dogs: Thoughts on Humans and Other Animals*. London: Granta.

Hallinan, J. T. 2009. *Why we Make Mistakes and What we Can do to Avoid Them*. London: Ebury.

Heidegger, M. [1926] 2010. *Being and Time*. Albany, NY: SUNY Press.

Heine, S. J., D. R. Lehman, E. Ide, C. Leung, S. Kitayama, T. Takata & H. Matsumoto 2001. "Divergent Consequences of Success and Failure in Japan and North America: An Investigation of Self-Improving Motivations and Malleable Selves". *Journal of Personality and Social Psychology* **81**(4): 599–615.

Hendricks, V. F. (ed.) 2004. *Feisty Fragments for Philosophy*. London: King's College London Publications.

Homer-Dixon, T. 2006. *The Upside of Down: Catastrophe, Creativity, and the Renewal of Civilization*. London: Souvenir.

Houellebecq, M. 1998. *Whatever*, P. Hammond (trans.). London: Serpent's Tail.

Jacobs, A. 2008. *Original Sin: A Cultural History*. London: SPCK.

Jacobs, J. 2001. *Choosing Character: Responsibility for Virtue and Vice*. Ithaca, NY: Cornell University Press.

Kearney, R. (ed.) 1984. *Dialogues with Contemporary Continental Thinkers*. Manchester: Manchester University Press.

Kurtz, P. 2010. *Exuberant Skepticism*. New York: Prometheus.

Lawton, G. 2011. "The Grand Delusion". *New Scientist* (14 May), 35–41.

Le Feuvre, L. 2010. "Introduction: Strive to Fail". In *Failure*, L. Le Feuvre (ed.), 12–21. London: Whitechapel Gallery.

LeVay, S. 2009. *When Science Goes Wrong: Twelve Tales from the Dark Side of Discovery*. London: Plume.

MacIntyre, A. 2007. *After Virtue: A Study in Moral Theory*, 3rd edn. Notre Dame, IN: University of Notre Dame Press.

Marcus, G. 2008. *Kluge: The Haphazard Construction of the Human Mind*. London: Faber.

Marcuse, H. 1987. *Eros and Civilisation: A Philosophical Inquiry into Freud*. London: Ark.

Marcuse, H. 1991. *One-Dimensional Man*. London: Routledge.

Maxwell, N. 2007. *From Knowledge to Wisdom: A Revolution for Science and the Humanities*, 2nd edn. London: Pentire.

McDermott, S. 2007. *How to be a Complete and Utter Failure in Life, Work and Everything*, 2nd edn. Harlow: Pearson.

McIntyre, L. 2006. *Dark Ages: The Case for a Science of Human Behavior*. Cambridge, MA: MIT Press.

Merleau-Ponty, M. 1962. *Phenomenology of Perception*. London: Routledge.

Moriarty, M. 2006. *Fallen Nature, Fallen Selves: Early Modern French Thought II*. Oxford: Oxford University Press.

Mulhall, S. 2005. *Philosophical Myths of the Fall*. Princeton, NJ: Princeton University Press.

Murphy, D. 2012. *The Architecture of Failure*. Winchester: Zero Books.

Nussbaum, M. C. 2001. *The Fragility of Goodness: Luck and Ethics in Greek Tragedy and Philosophy*. Cambridge: Cambridge University Press.

Ormerod, P. 2005. *Why Most Things Fail: Evolution, Extinction and Economics*. London: Faber.

Pensky, M. 2001. *Melancholy Dialectics: Walter Benjamin and the Play of Mourning.* Amherst, MA: University of Massachusetts Press.

Petroski, H. 1992. *To Engineer is Human: The Role of Failure in Successful Design.* New York: Vintage.

Pile, S. 2011. *The Ultimate Book of Heroic Failures.* London: Faber.

Pollard, J. 2005. "Authenticity and inauthenticity". In *Existential Perspectives on Human Issues: A Handbook for Therapeutic Practice*, E. van Deurzen & C. Arnold-Baker (eds), 171–9. Basingstoke: Palgrave Macmillan.

Poole, A. 2005. *Tragedy: A Very Short Introduction.* Oxford: Oxford University Press.

Pratt, O. T. & S. Dikkers 1999. *You are Worthless.* London: Boxtree.

Radcliffe Richards, J. 2000. *Human Nature After Darwin: A Philosophical Introduction.* London: Routledge.

Ricoeur, P. 1986. *Fallible Man,* rev. edn, New York: Fordham University Press.

Roberts, J. 2011. *The Necessity of Errors.* London: Verso.

Sandage, S. A. 2005. *Born Losers: A History of Failure in America.* Harvard, MA: Harvard University Press.

Sartre, J. P. 1958. *Being and Nothingness.* London: Routledge.

Schopenhauer, A. [1851] 1970. *Essays and Aphorisms.* London: Penguin.

Schulz, K. 2010. *Being Wrong: Adventures in the Margin of Error.* London: Portobello.

Shields, D. 2008. *The Thing About Life Is That One Day You'll Be Dead.* New York: Knopf.

Small, H. 2007. *The Long Life.* Oxford: Oxford University Press.

Smith, R. R. 2011. *Driving with Plato: The Meaning of Life's Milestones.* London: Profile.

Songe-Møller, V. 2002. *Philosophy Without Women: The Birth of Sexism in Western Thought.* London: Continuum.

Sorkin, A. R. 2010. *Too Big to Fail: Inside the Battle to Save Wall Street.* London: Penguin.

Spengler, O. [1922] 2006. *The Decline of the West.* New York: Vintage.

Spier, F. 2011. *Big History and the Future of Humanity.* Oxford: Wiley-Blackwell.

Stenger, V. J. 2008. *God: The Failed Hypothesis.* Amherst, NY: Prometheus.

Sternberg, R. J. (ed.) 2002. *Why Smart People Can Be So Stupid.* New Haven, CT: Yale University Press.

Tavris, C. & E. Aronson 2007. *Mistakes Were Made (But Not by Me): Why We Justify Foolish Beliefs, Bad Decisions, and Hurtful Acts.* London: Pinter & Martin.

Taylor, G. 2006. *Deadly Vices.* Oxford: Clarendon Press.

Tenembaum, Y. 2011. "The Success and Failure of Non-violence". *Philosophy Now* **85**, July/August: 34.

Thomas, L. 1988. *The Wonderful Mistake: Notes of a Biology Watcher.* Oxford: Oxford University Press.

Velleman, J. D. 1991. "Well-Being and Time". *Pacific Philosophical Quarterly* **72**: 48–77.

Weatherill, R. 1998. *The Sovereignty of Death.* London: Rebus.

Wilkinson, R. & K. Pickett 2009. *The Spirit Level: Why More Equal Societies Almost Always Do Better.* London: Allen Lane.

Wilson, F. 2011. *How to Survive the Titanic, or The Sinking of J. Bruce Ismay.* London: Bloomsbury.

Wittgenstein, L. 1967. *Philosophical Investigations.* Oxford: Blackwell.

Woodson, D. G. 2010. "'Failed' States, Societal 'Collapse,' and Ecological 'Disaster'". In *Questioning Collapse*, P. A. McAnany & N. Yoffee (eds), 269–98. Cambridge: Cambridge University Press.

Young, S. 2002. *Great Failures of the Extremely Successful: Mistakes, Adversity, Failure and Other Steppingstones to Success.* Los Angeles, CA: Tallfellow Press.

Zerzan, J. 2002. *Running on Emptiness: The Pathology of Civilization.* Los Angeles, CA: Feral House.

Index